# April Cornell at Home

To Nonna Jennie,
Enjoy!
April Cornell.

# April Cornell at Home

GLORIOUS PRINTS AND PATTERNS TO DECORATE
AND ENHANCE YOUR HOME

## April Cornell

*with original photography by Mick Hales*

*To Chris*
My husband and partner and in-everything collaborator—
who has been my man, my friend and my colleague. I dedicate
this book which is, of course, not mine—but *ours*.

To my sons, who have spent
their babyhoods in our arms,
on airplanes, trains and cars—in foreign cities
and at home—who have spent their childhoods
cavorting in shops
and hiding in changing rooms.
You have been the most loving of boys,
and are now the most elegant of men.
Thank you for making us live in the everyday,
for our precious time together
and for being with us on our family journey.

Conceived and Produced by
Glitterati Incorporated
225 Central Park West
New York, New York 10024
www.GlitteratiIncorporated.com

Design: lync.

First published in the United States of America in 2003 by Glitterati Incorporated

First edition, 2003

Hardcover ISBN 0-9721152-5-0

Printed and bound in China

# ACKNOWLEDGMENTS

Thank you to our customers for appreciating our style.
This book in words and pictures is truly for you.

Thank you to the following people
who made this book possible:

Marta Hallett and Ima Ebong for bringing us the idea.

Chris Cornell for seeing the potential and suggesting a structure.
Chris long wanted to do a book, and made sure this one happened.

My mother, Florence Janbroers and my mother-in-law, Mary Cornell,
for provoking my memory and for being sounding boards for the text.

Helene Hamel, designer, artist and champion of my vision, for
being a stickler for details and making sure we had the best book possible.

Mick Hales for being the most professional and agreeable
of photographers in the midst of a summer heat wave.

Lynne Yeamans for book design—several times!

Barbara Carpenter-Sawyer for attending to everyone's thirst
and hunger on those hot days with practical and cheerful grace.
And, to little Leandra, her constant companion.

Ruth Custodio for bringing her fine eye and hand to our rooms.

Alice Beisiegel for making my garden look its best and making
every flower arrangement enhance the setting.

Robin Gronlund for steering the ship and keeping us on schedule.

Beth Robinson for graphics compilation and coordination.

Lisa Mozo for proofing the text.

Harpreet Sindhu and the Delhi team for translating my vision into product.

Thank you everyone.

# Contents

# the way we live now

brown headed
cowbird

Almost thirty years ago, Chris and I stood in the early morning air of a spring day in northern Afghanistan, in a town called Serepol. We were at a river bend, on a small bridge with a stream flowing beneath it. I remember there was a threshing mill beside the stream. In the distance, through the haze of the early morning light, we could glimpse villagers walking down a long country road into town. It was a beautiful and ancient sight we would hold on to forever—a memory of place, custom and beauty.

We were in Serepol looking for finely woven kilim carpetbags. About a year earlier we had started our business, Cornell Trading, buying beautiful textiles from the East and carrying them back to Montreal to sell. Well off the beaten path, Afghanistan, at that time, was our personal treasure trove. We loved the rich colors of the carpets, the flowing, floral dresses of the nomadic women and the earthy richness of the people—a composite of beauty and atmosphere.

LEFT: *An old apple tree on the left, a flagstone walkway in the center and perennial plants pouring onto the path, create the framework for my flower garden. I have planted a pear tree in anticipation of the eventual demise of my apple tree. In the meantime, we enjoy the fragrant blossoms and abundant apples the old tree offers. Woodpeckers visit it frequently and our squirrels love the harvest.*

Kabul, the capital, was alive with young travelers just like us; bargaining, buying and trying their hand at business. For those who learn by doing, seeing, touching and tasting, a richer and more intimate basic business schooling would be hard to imagine. This hands-on experience formed the basic principles of our business.

Good product, fair dealing, and value for both the buyer and the seller; without this understanding, it would have been impossible to buy from the many craftsman and dealers in Afghanistan, and unlikely that we could have developed our business into what it is today.

Almost thirty years later, our love affair with textiles and design, travel and people has spawned into a business with headquarters in four countries (Canada, United States, India and China), and one hundred shops across North America. Together, we have developed a visual library of designs with references gleaned from our travels, home, and countries around the world.

LEFT: *Long summer days give Chris and I time to appreciate our northern garden. Here we are standing in front of the dried flower garden with the drying shed in the background.*

Our collections, ideas, abilities and our venues have grown over time. However, we have kept a constant measure by which we test our efforts and bring everything back to the beginning—to that Serepol morning. Everything must be beautiful. That is the first and basic tenet of my designing: begin with beauty and all other details will follow.

I was recently speaking to a regular customer in our Michigan store. She'd bought lots of our merchandise over the years and was telling me about it. Beside her stood her friend. I turned to her and said, "So, are you a regular customer?" "No," she smiled, "I'm just a beginner!" We all laughed. I was personally very charmed by the statement and continued to think about it for weeks afterwards.

A "beginner"—well, that's wonderful. She wants to start something new; she wants to begin. I liked that idea! But, also, in that self-description, I worried there was a feeling that she needed to acquire knowledge to use our product. I didn't like that. It seemed to me that there was a hint of nervousness, hesitation and indecision about what lay in front of her—decorating! I want my customers to feel comfortable with putting their own look together. I want them to enjoy it. It shouldn't in any way make you feel uptight or ill at ease or inexperienced—it should make you feel good. Think about eating ice cream for the first time—not too much experience required—just the desire to do it.

Chris and I are no longer the flower children of those days. We now have three grown sons, Cameron, Lee and Kelly. We live in Vermont in a big old house, not the small apartment where we started out in Montreal. We have spent our professional lives building a concept, an idea and a business that focuses on design and beautiful products.

In this book, we would like to show you how we put it all together in our own home, how we use nature as a guide, good memories as a reference point to build style and a happy atmosphere to bind it together and make it all worthwhile.

# bringing nature indoors

# The Whole Thing

periwinkle as a flower,

olive as a pointed leaf, China blue as imagined eyes,

peach reflecting the warmth of

the sun on fruit, faded blue as a tired sky,

haze seen through a mist, all the colors talk to me in

peaceful recognition. Petals then, and flower, become

artful layer of cream on ivory, rose on pink.

I bow to nature in my printed rose, and

take inspiration from this thing,

the world of color, the whole thing,

this world.

I start with my porch—the steps, the walkway, and my front door—from brick-red, wooden steps, to periwinkle pillars, the sage green balcony and wicker chairs, painted a sunny yellow color, the stage is set for nature to enter. See how the geraniums, which I love, climb the stairs, hemlocks wrap the porch, floral painted watering cans march up the steps, their extravagant blooms seeming to alight naturally on pretty cushions. Through this path, nature enters my home: first by its own natural means, and then through artful imitation in textiles and objects.

A porch is a place of welcome, a statement about the character and intention of the dweller within. Welcoming, it can be a friendly embrace, a cheerful hello to the street, as well as a warm and seemingly smiling atmosphere for visitors and family. I like to keep my front porch deliberately cheerful and welcoming.

Color, my reliable collaborator, sets the tone. Whether in prints and flowers, natural or on cushions, let nature's colors play a role. The color scheme of the exterior of our home is a Provence palette—periwinkle blue, sage green and straw yellow. When Chris and I thought about painting this big old house we were stymied—what colors to use? It was such a large canvas, such a statement, such an expression of ownership. What an opportunity!

After some false starts (I was going for red originally), I took out some of our old prints and

LEFT: *This artwork is the border of my "Autumn Hydrangea" print. It shows sprays of dried hydrangeas, wild indigo pods and an indigo bunting. These natural elements emphasize the concept of bringing nature into the home, through art and textiles.*

best color recipes, and found this favorite combination. What could be more right than nature?

A periwinkle sky, sage green like a soft forest, straw yellow for the window frame, and sunshine yellow for our old wicker chairs. (The red remained in the painted floorboards of the porch!). To give it the accents that make it all harmonize, I used strong color in the cushions, changing them every spring. I chose prints from our "Bloom" and "Petunia" collection. Potted geraniums complete the color story.

It is wonderful to bring nature indoors in the form of flowers and nature-inspired textiles. Nature's palette is a welcome sight in winter, when days are short and cold, and nights long and colder. Brilliant amaryllis cheer up a dark

wild indigo.

LEFT: *A summer day in the garden is an absolute godsend. I enjoy it for all it is worth. When I can't be outside, nature comes indoors, through flowers, and nature inspired textiles and objects.*

December; pots of hyacinths liven a gray January as do pussy willows in March—along with a flowered cloth on the table that says "spring will come." These are nature's representatives, her symbols that inspire us in the cold months. They are so important for visual nourishment, when all about lies quiet and bare.

Ah—but the warm months— the wonderful warm months, when days are long, and we move outside, meeting nature on her ground. These are great days for outdoor dining, garden parties, sitting on a swing, backyard picnics, sunset cocktails, barbecues, bird watching and gardening. This is when I bring my pretty things outdoors to meet nature at her best! A long row of cushions on the stone wall gives a unique seating arrangement for a casual outdoor party. Everyone can choose a seat to suit his or her taste; be it the plumpness of the pillow or color of the cushion. I place tables around the

patio, under the apple tree, near benches by the drying shed, or next to Adirondack wooden chairs on the lawn. Then I cover all the seating areas with a bounty of cushions and the tables with pretty cloths. I lay a blanket—nicely mellowed from years of use—on the grass where the babies can play. I invite the local birds to sing, and as they sing, I sit back and smell the roses. Really, the fragrance can be quite heady!

Outdoor entertaining has no rival; it is like throwing a party in the most exclusive of settings—nature. I take advantage of the free atmospherics provided by the air and sun, and nature's scents and sounds. I build on these elements by adding my own natural ingredients. A very flowery tablecloth (resplendent with blooms), whatever seasonal fruits are available (bowls of strawberries, blueberries, sliced watermelon) and a glass pitcher of tangy fresh-squeezed lemonade. In the early autumn, an apple pie or a bushel of apples might grace the table. All the good and yummy produce of the season finds its place at a garden party. Nothing compares to having fruit in-season—unless perhaps one picks it in the wild!

I even love it when it gets too hot—when I start to perspire and feel myself as one of nature's creations too! Responding physically to the sun and temperature, I appreciate the sweet moistness of a summer day; the dampness behind my neck, cotton blouses clinging softly

*Indigo bunting*

to my back, heavy hair tied with a ribbon—all these sensations form a memory of summer—summer in Vermont. It is a wonderful memory to carry into winter. It is an inspiration that is perfect for design. During the heady summer months, I assemble a treasure trove of palettes and motifs. The following winter, before the first snowdrops of spring have pushed their way up through slowly unfreezing ground, I surround myself with the exuberant color and blooms of that high summer harvest. Dried flowers decorate my home and print fabrics cover tables and chairs. On a particularly gray February day, I cut a rhododendron stalk from my snow-covered bush and nurture it in the warmth of my kitchen, until a powerful hot house bloom bursts forth.

LEFT: *I love the way these cushions follow the stone wall. It looks like a special seat has been placed for everyone at this garden party. A field of yellow coreopsis in the background tells the tale of high summer in the garden.*

## Notes from the Drying Shed

Thistle heads, golden yarrow, big bunches of hydrangea, fabulous sprays of blue statice, an assortment of garden tools, a woven willow basket and a Colombian pot, aged to quintessential artistry, create a veritable tableau. Really, just like a still life, these drying flowers from the garden are a thing of beauty.

This is a small wooden drying shed for flowers. When we bought our house the shed was a doghouse with metal fencing and a gravel-run in front. We don't have dogs, so we didn't need it as a doghouse, but it was such a charming building in need of a purpose. We painted it periwinkle with a sage trim, like the big house, and thought about it for a while. Alice Beiseigel, a Vermont gardener, and the true angel of my garden, suggested the idea of a dried flower shed. Perfect! Nature all-year-round. We started a small garden where a gravelled area had been, and except for a few major raids by our resident groundhog and company, we have an annual bounty I use for decorating whenever I entertain.

I can't seem to stop dual purposing everything! A delicate flower becomes a print; a dried flower shed becomes a harvest for decorating. I love finding uses for my passions; and I love it when my passions resonate with my customers. Truthfully, being able to weave the things I

# Plants of the Drying Shed

Achillea species — Yarrow

Allium sphaerocephalon — Drumstick Allium

Artemesia ludoviciana 'Silver Queen' — Wormwood

Asclepias incarnata — Swamp Milkweed

Asclepias tuberosa — Butterfly Weed

Astilbe species

Baptisia australis — False Indigo

Celosia spicata 'Flamingo Purple'; Celosia spicata 'Pink Candle'

Crambe cordifolia — Giant Kale

Echinops ritro — Globe Thistle

Eryngium 'Blaukappe' — Sea Holly

Gomphrena globosa — Globe Amaranth

Hydrangea paniculata 'Grandiflora Compacta'

Lavandula angustifolia — Lavender

Myrrhis odorata — Sweet Cicely

Nigella damascena — Love-in-a-mist

Polygonum cuspidatum — Japanese Knotweed

Rosa species

Stachys lanata — Lamb's Ears

appreciate into my designs—flowers, nature, art—has made my work tremendously fulfilling and interesting. This natural inspiration is the food of my design. It is also the connection that links us with our customers—it is the same "nature" loved by them . . . I mean, by you.

## Designing from Nature

The wild indigo plant, an indigo bunting (a blue bird of the forest) and autumn dried hydrangea were the natural components for this design. I first saw the indigo bunting from my office window in Williston, Vermont. If you are a birdwatcher, you will appreciate how the heart leaps at such a sight. The bird stayed around for a week or so and then was gone. That same year, in the fall, I went to our local farmers' market in Burlington and saw for the first time pails full of *Baptisia australis*, or what someone there told me was wild indigo. Sounds and names affect me greatly, and this wild indigo, with its beautifully tapered dark navy seedpods,

*LEFT: These flower-strewn plaids reflect the colors of an autumn garden. Nature is a good guide for combining color and I imitate her colors in design to bring the feel of the fall indoors.*

*BELOW: I like to change my cushion covers frequently, greeting the new season with appropriate colors. This collection is called "Birdsong." It is full of birds of a tropical garden.*

made mental harmony with my other new friend—the indigo bunting! I needed just one more element to fill the frame of my new print design; delicate autumn hydrangeas, as fine as parchment and as delicately colored, were plentiful in the market that fall—I had found my missing ingredient! I added them to the mix, and that is how my hydrangea print design was conceived. To keep the naturalist element in the design, I wrote the names autumn hydrangea and wild indigo in notebook style by hand on the print. To acknowledge my two cultural references (Canada and the United States) I wrote the name in French—"*indigo sauvage.*" Well, nature definitely got in the door that time! The next year I planted wild indigo at the office (great for dried flower arrangements) and hydrangeas at home. I am still waiting for that indigo bunting to return.

# every fabric tells a story

# PRAKASH'S PALATIAL TANDOORI PANEER

*(Serving on a silver tray, adds flavor to the everyday)*

1 pound (500g) fresh paneer
2 tablespoons of chat masala

2 fresh tomatoes

Green peppers

3 tablespoons fresh cream

2 onions

1 tablespoon ginger paste

1 tablespoon garlic paste

1 tablespoon lemon juice

6 tablespoons of yogurt

Cut paneer in to small (1") cubes.

Chop onion and green pepper into squares; mix with above items in a large dish.

Stir and chill for 30 minutes. Bake in hot oven until brown. Serve with lime soda and watch your party take off!

# A Little Bit of How To...

## Start with Color

I always start with color in designing my prints—a collection has to have color. In any given collection, there is always a primary print that encompasses all of the colors in that range. The main print is always a floral design and has at least eight colors in it. The colors of the primary print are reflected to varying degrees in coordinating fabrics comprised of stripes, checks, small-scale prints, plaids and jacquards.

The different patterns form the secondary pieces of a collection. All the fabrics in a given collection are designed to work together; they all match, because the colors have all been pulled from the same palette. Whether designing a print or decorating, the principles are similar and fairly simple to follow—find a palette you like and work within it.

If the decorating project is big enough (say an entire room), be sure to include different fabric textures: contrast a chenille blanket with a cotton bedcover, or jacquard napkins with a printed tablecloth, or mix nubbly with smooth fabrics. Experiment with different textures. Have fun with shapes, too. Cushions, for example, can be round, oblong, square, oversized, or undersized. Using contrasting shapes and tex-

BELOW: *I keep a collection of cushions at hand to throw on the bed or add a little extra comfort to a reading chair. Each one is unique and charming.*

tures adds a touch of individuality. My cushions have some fun names, designed to amuse and to inspire—"Puffettas" are round and flat; "Luxurettas" are over-the-top rectangles; "Bon-Bon" is a bolster with ruffled ends—it looks like a giant candy; "Ruchetta" has ruched (strips of fabric evenly gathered and sewn together in a repeat pattern) details; and "Muffin" is a quilted pad for kitchen chairs. "Julietta," "Ophelietta"—the names are as varied as our styles. We have fun with cushions, and I just love throwing the extras from my bed in a heap on the floor at night. It is such a feeling of luxury and decadence.

Here are some tips to coordinating a space no matter the style you prefer:

### USE SCALE

*large and small size prints in the
same color family.*

### USE SOLIDS

*jacquards, velvets and silks with standout
detailing. Use pleating, pin tucking,
fine piping, or pretty buttons, to make solid
fabrics more interesting.*

### USE CONTRAST

*stripes, polka-dots and plaids work well
as foils for your print story.*

### USE EMBROIDERY

*especially on napkins, cushions, runners,
throws, blankets, pillows and sheets.
Highlight colors from your palette with
embroidered accents.*

### MIX OLD WITH NEW

*enjoy mixing old favorites with new
purchases. Vintage or family treasures
usually fit right in with our product.
I draw so much on vintage references
and we use so much fine needlework in our
own collections, that old and new
are at home together.*

### USE WHITE

*especially for bedding; add crisp white cotton
or linen cushions with some embroidery
handwork on them to lighten prints and add
elegance to your bed.*

Add some three dimensional elements so things aren't too soft and droopy—a metal vase, a wooden bowl and silver napkin rings all add a necessary firmness to a look. Use natural surfaces. Place a breakfast cloth in a diamond shape on a rectangular table, allowing wooden corners to show, for example. A wood, brass, or iron bed frame provides a good contrast to the "dressing" on the bed. A wooden chair or bench nearby can do the same job.

When it comes to windows, there is always the question of whether to dress or not to dress. Your own home will tell you if you need a wall of curtain fabric to hide the view outside, give privacy or create an environment. Focus on your curtains as an important decorating element. On the other hand, if your window is the vehicle for sunlight to spill in, you may choose not to have curtains at all. Sheer curtains, such as see-through voiles, pretty organdies and glimmering tissue can all provide mood while still giving translucence. In contrast, thick velvets mixed with brocades give a rich and private look. Most of all, enjoy the experience of deciding on the right look for your window—nobody is right all the time. Allow yourself the freedom of a few experiments; sometimes the results will be more pleasurable and satisfying than a carefully thought out plan. I have had people buy our curtains to use as tablecloths, and our table-cloths to use as curtains. I have even seen our honeycomb tea towels hemmed and hung as café curtains in a country kitchen. It is your home and your belongings!

# California Softness

*ivory blush*

*soft sage*

*mellow plaid*

## Travels in Cloth

When I talk about inspiration from a place, I mean the colors, the atmosphere and the attitude of that particular place. These elements impact me visually.

When I think of California, I think of a sky that is wide, flat and grey blue. I think of golden yellow stalks—a dull yellow—mingled with grass, the color of sage green. I think of the sun—a mellow sun—and an ocean that is blue; not a brilliant blue, but a soft, smoky Cadet-blue. This is what I call a palette, in this case, my California palette. I use these colors in my prints—to decorate and to create an atmosphere with a soft California feel, a big sky feel. This is what California does to me—it gives me its color.

# California

*smoky blue*

I visit California frequently. I can't remember the streets, the location of shops, or restaurants that I've visited a dozen times, but I do remember the atmosphere. The sight of an intensely involved couple in a trendy restaurant—being served the hippest culinary menu "du jour." The couple sits wrapped up in each other, looking at each other—they're in the middle of an atmosphere and that, I do remember, is the California style.

*grass green*

*sage green*

# Portugal Terracotta

Portugal is a beautiful place. It is craggy, rocky and stony. It has country villages and seaside towns and plenty of fish. Portugal is simpler and earthier than Spain or Italy. What I get from Portugal is its rich, earthy, terracotta colors. Everywhere, from the walls to pots, there is every shade of terracotta imaginable—red earth and rusts, corals and oranges—all bathed in golden sunlight. Call it Portuguese sunrise, call it Portuguese morning, call it a Portuguese palette. For me, the sun-warmed colors of Portugal include beautiful rich corals, warm golds and yellows. I use these

*orange*

*gold*

# Portugal

sunny yellow

olive

red earth

colors continuously—in prints, paint, walls, cupboards, cups and plates. These are warm colors, flattering to the skin. Sit in a room painted in a Portuguese coral and you will look prettier and healthier.

Porto is a beautiful old city in the north of Portugal with a wonderful old restaurant district. One night Chris, his brother, John, and I had dinner at a small fish restaurant in Porto. We made our way inside, past an already crowded ground floor, upstairs to a small room filled with diners. It was noisy and warm, even though it was November.

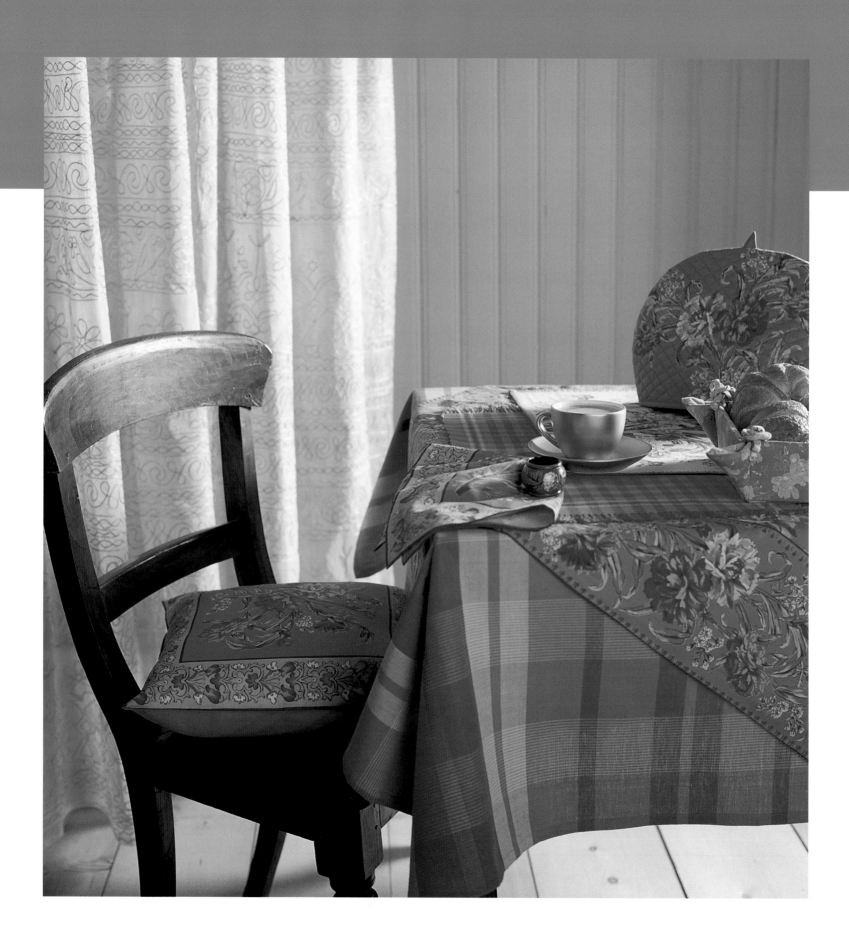

*retro brown*

*terracotta*

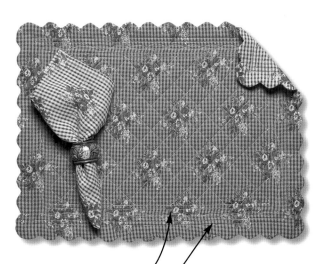

*dark green*

*dark red*

As the room became more crowded, the temperature rose and voices grew louder. Local wines were served and the smell of fresh fish permeated the air—it was the atmosphere of Porto, the warm earthy atmosphere of Portugal, of a Portuguese evening. This lively and entertaining spirit is a scene etched in my memory—the spirit of the place, its style, its attitude, the way of enjoyment—and one I use as a reference in my design work. I draw on those ideas in my own entertaining and in trying to create an atmosphere of conviviality in my home or at a party.

# Boreal Forest Canopy

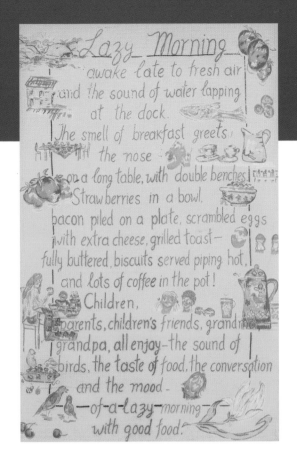

Do you know where the Boreal Forest is? It is a huge wooded area that sweeps across northern Canada and comprises seventy percent of forestland. It has its own ecology and starts north of the forty-ninth parallel and reaches all the way to where the trees dwindle out. It is full of birch and big old hemlocks, spruces, balsams and maple trees. In open spaces, trilliums, black-eyed Susans and carpets of tiny wood violets can be found in the summer. It is also the summer home for many woodland warblers.

crimson

golden yellow

*gold*

*maple*

*rust*

It is a place where Chris and I and the family go every summer. On a secret lake, without a road, we go by boat to an old house without electricity, but with plenty of hurricane lamps and propane lights. We come here for peace and quiet—to unwind, replenish our energies and play as a family on this soft and quiet lake. Surrounding us are colors that inspire me. In many ways, the colors of the Boreal Forest are shared by the Adirondack Mountains to the south. If you know the colors of the Adirondacks, you will be familiar with these palettes.

*golden yellow*

*rust*

There are greens as dark, dense and blue as an old fir tree, and as fresh as an uncurling fern; there are blues as deep as a lake and as bright as a summer sky, and golds the color of black-eyed Susans and birch leaves in the fall. A blanket of maple leaves yields reds, rusts and brilliant oranges. Imbue all this with an atmosphere of big family breakfasts, lazy days on the dock, crisp nights under quilts and you have an atmosphere that adds richness to the Boreal Forest palette, creating an atmosphere that resonates with memories of good times.

# Provence Sun and Sky

*yellow*

*azure blue*

*cobalt blue*

Provence is the South of France. Far from sophisticated Paris lies a region famous for its color. Do you know I have never been to Provence? Never felt its yellow sun or brilliant blue sky, but somehow, when I combine blue and yellow, the word Provence just speaks for itself. Another way to say Provence is: yellow sun, blue sky.

*provence yellow*

*buttercup yellow*

## Provence

I have based several designs on Provence colors: one is brilliant yellow and cobalt blue; another, I call winter Provence, has more golds and smoky blues; and a third, is lemon yellow and soft periwinkle. All of these colors look beautiful in the morning—kitchens take blue and yellow beautifully and a Provence bedroom is pure sunshine. It's a happy color. And for those of us who have never been to Provence—here it is!

*indigo blue*

# India Jewel Tones

*jewel tones*

Jaipur is a city in northwestern India. It is known as the "pink city" because its walls are made of pink sandstone. The phrase "pink city" certainly stirs the imagination. This is the city of Maharajahs and Maharanis, of richness, color, and jewels. When I think of Jaipur I think of the rich color of princely jewels, the brilliant multi-colored saris of Rajasthani women and fantastic tie-dyed turbans. I also think of precious stones—rubies, emeralds, sapphires and turquoise—and lacings of silver and gold embroidery, woven in precious cloth. I think of a camel fair in Pushkar, with camel dealers and races, and stacks of saddles and camel headgear: embroidered, tasseled ornamental crowns for these beautiful beasts of burden of the desert.

alizarin crimson

dark sapphire

I remember a cup of sweet tea—a small cup of "Chai," thick, milky, deliciously sweet tea—shared over a stack of handwoven blankets. I also remember the hazy dust-filled air, and the tented shop of a salesman—a handsome, mustachioed Rajasthani, with a tumbling turban. This scene has inspired a hundred print designs in a thousand different color combinations. I go back to it again and again, mimicking its richness, its decorative boldness—its theatricality. From this "luxouriousity" I draw the pinks, the reds, the jewel tones and the rich and flamboyant brocades of our collection.

# Nova Scotia Blueberry

To me, Nova Scotia represents an emotion as big as my parents—both of whom were born there (as well as my many aunts and uncles and grandparents). The essence of Nova Scotia can also be found in the perfection of its patches of wild blueberries. Have you looked in a blueberry bush? I mean, really peered closely at a wild patch? Blueberries are a seduction of blues—dusty and powdery, soft or smoky, deep as navy, or a pink-tipped periwinkle blue—mixed with the sharp green of small, unripened berries. This Nova Scotia-inspired blueberry palette is one of our favorites. It seems to have universal appeal and is among our most popular colors. People replenish their selection of blue linens year after year, adding the latest version of our Nova Scotia-inspired hues to their collection.

One more blue we've added to our palette is called "China Blue," the color of those Cape Bretoners' eyes. When my son Lee was small, one of his nicknames was blueberry, the result of his round, blue eyes. "Just like his great Grammy," we said.

The Cape Bretoners of Nova Scotia are a romantic lot, many of them can weave a tale, or sing a song to pull your heart, or scare you out of your seat. Like the mournful Scots from whom they descend, they enjoy a good cry—and that's one more way of saying "blue."

*navy blue*

# Paris à la Crème

rose pink

blush pink

baby blue

mint green

soft peach

crème fraiche

Another French reference for me is Paris—now here I have traveled dozens of times! I love the cafés, the patisseries and architecture. I love the bridges that span the Seine, and the walkways below the bridges. I love the St.-Germain back streets and the church of St.-Germain-des-Prés. I love the Marais with its narrow streets and stone walls that open onto courtyards.

One night, Chris and I were walking in Paris, in the St.-Germain area, looking for a restaurant. We peered through a stone-arched window and saw a jazz bar cum restaurant that went straight to our hearts. The round tables were covered with heavy-fringed table shawls. Russian? Polish? Czechoslovakian prints? I know not what they were, but they were pure Bohemian and made a Parisian fantasy for us.

We have recalled this scene many times when trying to communicate the magic of Paris. Somehow, when I think of Paris, I think of the color pink—though Paris can be woefully gray and cloudy—it's the pink of the frosting and the sweetness of the pastries that impress me!

espresso

bistro

café en Paris

One of my designs is called "Tea Time" or *"L'heure du thé"* and is drawn straight from a French patisserie. While walking in Paris, I spotted a pretty pastry shop. I went in, and eyed the display case. Everything looked so good. There were *petit fours*, *éclairs*, and tartlets filled with fruits; there were also various drinks of Limonette, herbal tea and lemonade. It was all so stimulating! I quickly bought one of each pastry and started photographing them for reference. The owner watched disapprovingly as I noted down the delightful descriptions from his menu—*café*, *l'heure du thé*, *poire d'Anjou* and so on. I didn't improve the French impression of Americans, as I left with only a bite out of my *millefeuille* and a taste of my *cornet de crème*.

However, with the addition of some fresh fruits and berries of the season, I had a new print I named "Tea Time," decorated in frosty sweet pinks and greens—it is decadently sweet and decidedly French—*Paris à la crème.*

*sweet pinks*

*pink frosting*

# Southern Peaches and Cream

*sunny yellow*

*coral*

When I say southern I really mean Georgia; and when I say Georgia, I really mean to say peaches. For me, our "Southern" palette is all about the color peach and the softness of a peach itself. Like a peach turning to the sun, it is yellow, it is golden, it is reddish; it is peach. The blend of these colors is so sublime in nature. I try to capture it in my prints and linens, and in old-fashioned stripes and cabbage roses. I tease out this "Southern" peach palette. "Southern," is also about old-fashioned values and timeless traditions. It's about politeness and etiquette. It's about comfort, afternoon tea and hospitality. But it is also about dreamy lagoons, bayous and Spanish moss. It's about gators and turtles and diving birds. But, mostly, for me, it's about peach—the Georgia peach.

# around my rooms

# The House

be it a manor or a hut —
a camp, chalet or riverboat —
a student loft, a Vermont farm,
or, an understated prairie croft...
— these all our dwellings are —
a place to sleep, to rest our heads
to contemplate in comfort from our beds,
the thoughts and issues of each day.

to feel at home within our walls —
the separate world we have installed.

— to share with friends,
and those we know —
the feast of table and of soul.
— so when we open our front door,
a place of beauty beckons forth.

# Living with Beautiful Things

I think that in today's world the best a home can be is a solace and a balm for busy people to find refuge and spiritual replenishment. If you think of your house as you would food—as nourishment for your spirit and your mind and your creativity—then you must fill it with good things. Things that are good for your spirit and mind, that soothe and inspire you and that complement you and reinforce who you and your family are.

I don't think of my home simply as a space to be decorated; I think of it as living with beautiful things. Having placed this poetic license on decorating, I can offer some practical tips on how to achieve this ideal in your home.

The main feature of any room—the bed in your bedroom; the cupboards in your kitchen; or the table in your dining room—are all good places to begin decorating on a small scale. However, the largest and most dominating feature of any room is the walls and ceiling. They are often ignored, and yet, they present the biggest opportunity to make an impact with color. What a generous canvas—or some might say, "What potential for the wrong choice!"

I do understand the desire to choose a safe neutral color—one that you can live with and one that harmonizes with your belongings—

BELOW: *Pretty honeycomb hand towels, a tiny bouquet of golden runniculus and bachelor's buttons, with a blue drinking glass are simple touches, yet are visual elements that make a strong impact in the guest bathroom.*

but does neutral always need to say beige? Think of how color can make sallow complexions glow—how it can breathe new life into a dreary background—how it can lift even the dreariest spirits on a rainy day. Is it really "safe" to be neutral—to be only moderately happy with your home? Here are a few neutral colors April Cornell style—they are my own version of "safe" and all meet the following criteria:

- *Flatter people's skin tones, making them look happier and healthier*
- *Lift the spirits*
- *Add mood and ambience*
- *Complement my fabrics and furnishings and serve as a good background for our colorful prints*
- *All can easily be changed by repainting!*

## Corals:

Anything in this family is wonderfully flattering for both the living rooms and bedrooms. Choose soft, pinky corals, beautiful rich terracottas, and any shade in between. This color range has been a "safe" color for me over and over again. If you want to understand the impact of color, take a photo of people in a room painted white and contrast it with a room with color. See how much the wall color contributes to the décor—it is an important decorating feature.

## Yellows:

A sunny yellow like the one we use for our living room wall is a good bet. This room was actually very dark. Our living room is surrounded by massive trees, and receives little sunlight; changing the wall color to yellow (actually a cream and two yellows sponged together) made it much brighter and livelier. The effect feels as if the sun has filled the room. The wood detailing painted off-white highlights the coffered ceiling, the doorframes, the floor skirting and paneled doors. I normally use a soft white for all wood work.

## Greens:

Green goes well with so many things. Soft sages will work with most fabrics; nearly every print has some green in it, particularly florals with leaves. Prints that don't have green in them often

RIGHT: *This bed has a true "Nova Scotia" blue palette. I love mixing up textures and patterns. Checks, prints and stripes when in the same palette combine well together. The bedside table, coincidentally, also hails from Nova Scotia.*

contrast well with green. Add a little yellow to sage green and you can get into the olive family. Olive hues work well with dark woods and earthy, wine colors. A sharp apple green, like the color of our library, makes a tiny room a jewel.

These are my three "safe" colors for walls. They are safe because they answer the call for beauty, inspiration, and ambience. So play it "safe" and try a little color.

## Bedrooms

Our home is a three-story Colonial revival manse house with a tremendous amount of period woodwork. The most elaborate woodwork is on the ground floor and staircase. Much simpler wood detailing can be found on the second floor and plain Adirondack-style detailing decorates the third floor. The third floor serves as our sons' headquarters (they call it their "crib"). Two sons have left home now, so our third son, Kelly, reigns supreme on the third floor. There are no photos of this floor in the book!

I like my guest bedroom to feel special. Your guests should feel that you are happy to have them and that you care and are aware of what it is like to be in someone else's home. In my guest bedroom, I like to have a bedside light, fresh flowers, cotton sheets and an amplitude of pretty cushions

LEFT: *Fine crochet work framing the patchwork squares of this duvet is the element that brings this bedroom scene peacefully over the top. Late afternoon sunlight streams through the window, adding to the peaceful scene.*

on the bed with soft pillows at the head. The "sumptuousity" of the bed—an extra blanket for those northern winters, plus two quilts, really say, please stay! Add a chair for sitting or to throw a robe over, paper and pencil for midnight notes and a variety of books from humorous to philosophical. When you go to someone's home, don't you like to feel expected?

The centerpiece of another bedroom is an iron Birdsong bed with bird and vine motifs woven into the framework—bringing nature indoors. The patchwork quilt bedcover has a pretty summer palette of yellow and aqua. Small prints such as ginghams, multi-colored plaids and playful polka-dots form a patchwork that combines nostalgic elements with a casual contemporary cheerfulness. These playful elements keep the décor from being too serious. I love vintage fabrics but I do not want things to feel too precious or too worked. There should be joy within an environment. Leave room for today's needs and for family tchochkes as well as collectibles. The cushions are covered with a mix of fabrics, some based on the quilted bedcover and others drawn from old favorites. See the pretty melon-colored appliqué cushions on the chair and bed? They were handmade in Rajasthan and are favorites from a previous collection. Sometimes a room may need a complete makeover and it is worth retaining old cushions or blankets; these items from the past give character and history to a home, while marching forward with new decorating schemes.

Often, an array of cushions can help to change the look of an entire room. The introduction of a different color palette for cushions, for example, can be used to mark the changing seasons. Decorating with textiles is probably one of the easiest and least costly ways of transforming a room. In this bedroom, the bed and the color of the bedding dictate the look and feel of the room. See how the flowers and vase pick up the color of the bedding to complete the visual story.

Cobalt blues, periwinkles, and sunny yellows from my Provence collection are combined to make a cheerful guest bedroom. Flower strewn prints, ticking stripes, and hand embroidery on cushions and quilts make for a color palette that is uplifting. Although there are many different patterns on this bed, they all share a common color theme. Sometimes the yellow dominates and sometimes blue takes over; sometimes the key element is the print design, and at other times it is a texture that stands out, as in the case of the looped-yarn meadow embroidery on the cushion in the foreground. The sheer variety of color and texture make this bedroom feel individual and personal, yet also pleasing and harmonious. Items collected on various travels that are full of personal memories contribute to the

ABOVE: *The variety of ingredients in a room makes it feel special. Here, a hand-crocheted throw will be the "pièce de résistance" at the foot of the bed. The old tin mirror from Santa Fe adds an unusual touch.*

RIGHT: *In my blue bedroom, an ironware bed and table and an old metal-framed mirror with dusty aqua shade patina give a common language to this room. The pretty metal vase beside the bed picks up on the same theme. The blue bedding in heavy cotton satin is offset by the crisp whiteness of the pillowcases and sheets. Blue irises pick up the color theme and a wonderful knitted blue cushion emphasizes the color palette on the bed. I find using a touch of white in sheets and pillowcases adds a crisp clean quality to the bed. It also acts as a good foil or relief for my patterns.*

BELOW: *Chris and I read every night before we go to sleep—I feel lost without a book! A few good books beside a bed make a guest feel at home too.*

warmth of the room. A French Canadian bed-side commode serves as the backdrop for a small display of items that include silver buttons from India, enamel and silver treasure boxes from my sister and an Indian miniature painting that was purchased in Udaipur. The cream tulips come from my garden. The "where" and "who" of these treasures make them more conversational and supportive to the personality of the guest room.

Chris and I share a common aesthetic. We haven't embraced modern or postmodern styles—stark lines and colors don't engage us. However the classic beauty and lines of Victorian, British Colonial, Arts and Crafts and Art Nouveau styles inspire us. We interpret these periods in our own way, adding fresh color or practical, informal features that go with today's lifestyle. Naïve art is a favorite and I incorporate elements of it in my décor: a handmade wooden bowl, Haitian art and a child's painting all add to the elegant simplicity of a room. All these diverse references seem to work well together. I am not a purist where different periods are concerned, but I am an absolutist about beauty and style.

Our master bedroom opens onto a balcony and has shuttered windows covered with bamboo blinds. I love the filtered light that the adjustable blades of the wooden shutters give to the room. Facing west, the bedroom is espe-cially pretty in the late afternoon when the sunlight slants in. On the bed is a patchwork duvet in soft peach, ecru and melon colors. I call this collection "Peaceful Day," the palette is so soothing and restful. Cushions in assorted shapes add interest and humor. Each cushion shape has a different name: "Puffetta," "Fanetta," "Ruchetta," "Muffetta," "Tuffetta," and "Bon-Bon" (like a candy)—these shapes always make me smile. An old, French Canadian pine dresser and a well-worn mahogany-colored leather armchair are complementary furniture elements that enhance the natural look and feel of my bedroom.

## The Well-Dressed Bed

A well-dressed bed is an important element that adds finish to bedroom décor. I have a few simple standards that I follow when making a bed. I never cover the pillows. They are so pretty and are definitely there to be admired. Do not pull the blanket over the pillows, instead, let them sit on top of the bed.

The first step is to arrange the under layer of cotton sheets, then the pillows sitting pretty on top—for pillow covers use white crochet, or maybe white with embroidered details, or white cotton with a print border—but generally white pillows (ecru is an option, too) are best. I fold my top sheet, the edge of which may be crocheted or embroidered, over my quilt or duvet. Our bedding is reversible and I often pull back the duvet or quilt with a very generous fold, using five to six inches of sheet. This allows you to off set the contrasting print or plaid fabric of the duvet against crisp white pillows and sheets. If the sheet has a pretty crochet border, scalloped edges or embroidery, it will stand out even more, when juxtaposed against a duvet or quilt cover. Did I mention cotton? Sheets and pillowcases must be cotton! Next, I add cushions with different shapes. The cushion fabric may be drawn from matching color-coordinated prints, or from prints and plaids that are the reverse of the color combinations of the quilt. I like to throw in at least one odd element to add an unexpected visual surprise to the bed. In this case, a knitted cushion or a different fabric such as brocade or velvet provides contrasting texture. I also use solid cushions in colors that are reflected in the quilt and other embroidered cushions strewn about the bed.

On a queen-size bed, I use four pillows—two white and two colored—along with two to four extra cushions with assorted shapes. Make sure that at least two of the extra cushions match; it shouldn't look totally random. At the foot of the bed I place a crochet blanket, it could be new or vintage. Alternatively, a second quilt, folded at the foot of the bed is also a nice touch. If a second quilt is added to the foot of the bed, place a throw on a nearby chair as a

BELOW: *I like a well-dressed bed. The mix of textures and patterns are made harmonious by the teal and blue palette.*

visual link. The second quilt, should be a different texture—maybe velvet, or soft cotton voile. These supple fabrics provide a lovely "touchability" to the bed, making it inviting to snuggle inside. Texture is very important for a bed; nobody is more sensitive than during sleep. Everything should be a soft caress, which is why you should use cotton sheets. As a finishing touch, I usually add a cushion from our "Foot of the Bed" collection; alternatively, any color coordinated cushion that enhances the bedding can also be used. No room left on the bed for all those cushions? Put one on a nearby chair. The only other must-have for me is a pair of cozy slippers on the floor.

LEFT: *"Mi casa," as Chris describes our home, needs to be comfortable enough for all my men folk—three sons and a husband! In proportion, it needs to be ample and comfortable, and in style both rich and feminine to satisfy both of our tastes. I think the generous proportions of the furniture in this room (including the television!) combined with the opulent brocades of the upholstery do just that.*

## Living Room

We really use our living room as our family room. There are four men in the family: Chris and our sons, Cameron, Lee and Kelly. This calls for "man-sized" furniture—large, comfortable double-size chairs, a big coffee table and an oversized Ottoman, all pay homage to those who live there. As Chris says, "I always loved *mi casa*" ("and still do!"). *Mi casa* should feel like home.

Chris and I first met when I was eighteen and impressionable! I remember my first visit to his upstairs apartment on St. Marc Street in Montreal. I was floored when I saw this red-haired, bearded guy's—who I'd just fallen for—pretty funky apartment. This was not your average student apartment with obligatory orange crates in sight. Instead, old, French Canadian pine tables, dressers in rich golden pine and oxblood-stained tables served as Chris's college décor. Now, that will get a girl! To this day, we still have a lot of French Canadian furnishings in our home. The warm color of old pine, the soft shape of its thick boards and the beautifully turned legs of the tables go well with our style. We collect pieces we love from all over the world.

Our living room windows are dressed with tissue or gossamer-like curtains woven with "old gold" metallic thread, which soften the windows without blocking the light. The

stained-glass window from Montreal. It echoes the stained-glass elements found throughout the house and allows for a window treatment without curtains! I'm not big on curtains, especially when it's only nature looking in, but I would be lavish with them if I lived in New York City.

The ceiling light is from Montreal; its "Hall of Fame" fixture (love the description) was bought at Grand Central, an antique lighting store, in Old Montreal. The small wooden side table is from Nova Scotia and the collages are by my mother-in-law, Mary Cornell. She is primarily a floral watercolor artist but she works with collage for city scenes.

ample, masculine scale of the furniture is given a more romantic and feminine quality with an assortment of fine brocade fabrics used as upholstery and cushions.

## The Library

"Library," sounds like such a grand word. My library is actually a small cozy sitting room set off from the main living area. The library has four armchairs and a wall of bookshelves. It has a telephone, three reading lamps, small tables cluttered with objects and just large enough for a cup of coffee and a notepad. Framed within the main window is a smaller

A painting by Montreal artist, Ingrid Harrison, evokes strong memories of the city Chris and I lived in so many years ago. The painting depicts Montreal's back lanes and takes us back to the old days, to an apartment we once lived in on Bagg Street, in Montreal's East End. It is an area where different immigrant groups have settled for decades, in the process opening neighborhood bakeries, delicatessens, butcher shops and groceries. Our old apartment was a one roomer on top of a monument factory. Tombstone making would often continue until late at night. The décor of our Bagg Street apartment was decidedly on the casual side, full of wonderful Mexican blankets and Alpaca throws— precursors to future treasures. The memory of those early years drew us to the painting.

The items in our library: the old lamp, the stained-glass window and my favorite pine table all have a dual purpose. As decorative objects they are remarkably similar; all are handmade and use authentic materials such as old brass, pine and beautiful paper. These objects resonate well with each other and support the traditional look of the library. Everything is stylistically well integrated. Equally important is the added value these collectibles represent— as they resonate with our personal history. The old stained-glass comes from our birthplace— Montreal. The Nova Scotia table is from the

RIGHT: *Hurricane lamps add romance and a touch of practicality to the home. I love this lamp for its finely etched pattern on the glass and the soft green patina of the heavy brass base.*

beloved province of my grandparents. The collages by my mother-in-law evoke a sense of her presence in our home. The painting of a Montreal alley takes us back to our first apartment, while the painting by Vermont artist, Jane Horner, gives us a sense of the present— where our lives are now. Not all life can be lived in memory, but memories can contribute great atmosphere to a home. In our library, past and present work together, giving added value to our daily lives.

The added value of personal memories is a feature that is underplayed in decorating. When enough of the items in your home have added

RIGHT: *The Rumford fireplace in its own nook with benches on either side provides a separate conversation corner. We use it, particularly during parties, when serving a buffet meal. Guests can sit here for more intimate chats.*

LEFT: *Eclectic would be a fair description of our style. Stuffed armchairs, a cane plantation chair and a painted Brazilian bench all hum nicely together.*

*In the background, a Victorian style chesterfield contributes yet another layer of diversity. For an eclectic look like this to be successful it requires at least three distinctly different elements to work.*

RIGHT: *A library can be a grand reading room, a simple shelf of novels or a stack of three favorite books. I think it's best when it's personal—full of favorite authors, book friends, thoughts, humor and ideas. I use my books mainly for relaxation. And these friends are patient enough to wait for me at any time!*

value, there will be a personality and presence in your home that is all yours. I would not suggest decorating a home solely with objects of sentimental value; you should be discriminating and let go of things that you don't care for, or that don't fit in with your present environment. However, it is a true bonus to surround yourself with items that are beautiful and meaningful.

LEFT: *Our kitchen is the focal point of the house. The coral color creates a warm atmosphere conducive to conversation and lingering over food.*

BELOW: *One of my favorite holiday activities is baking. Family recipes that were passed on to me, I continue to pass on to friends. Here I am starting on my grandmother's shortbread cookie recipe.*

## Kitchen and Dining Area

Peach, coral and apricot are the warm and pleasing colors of my country-style kitchen. The cabinets, with their thick moldings and ceramic knobs, look like an armoire straight out of an old-fashioned French pastry shop. Plate rails, Portuguese marble for the counter top and a checkerboard ceramic tile floor, are permanent design elements in my kitchen. A butler's pantry set off to the side features glass-front cabinets in which I display all the crockery and glassware I love. Everything, from my grandmother's everyday dishes to our own painted mix-and-match ceramics and pretty champagne flutes are there for all to see. I love

to see all my pretty things on display. They contribute to the daily enjoyment of life. I feel that if one makes the effort to serve food— shop, select and prepare it—it is worth the extra effort to select pretty tableware, such as cotton napkins or a shapely glass. These elements add so much more value and respect to the effort. How do you make your efforts appear effortless? Fill your cupboards only with beautiful things—banish what you don't truly enjoy. Then anytime you put your hand in the cupboard only things you love will be there. A pretty bowl elevates a sliced banana and turns an every day meal into a special occasion. Likewise,

BELOW: *This is a collection of boldly hand painted pottery.*

RIGHT: *This old Manitoba pine hutch houses a collection of some of my truly favorite ceramics— old Chinese teapots and trays on the bottom shelf, Portuguese fruit plates and vintage glassware on the next two shelves, and lively painted café au lait cups on the top shelf.*

a shapely glass will transform mere orange juice into God's nectar and a woven basket will put meaning back into ordinary sliced bread! The trays and platters that decorate the kitchen and line the plate rail of my dining room come off the shelf regularly for frequent use. I'm not saving anything for the special occasion—I'm treating *all* occasions as special.

I am not a tremendous cook, but I do love to bake. On a quiet Sunday afternoon I find nothing more therapeutic than pulling out an old family recipe for tea biscuits, or scones, berry pies or shortbread cookies and going through all the familiar rituals of baking.

**plum loaf**

(capebreton tea bread)

dissolve a packet of yeast in scalded milk, add ½ molasses, 2 melted shortening, 2 raisins, add flour, let rise until double in bulk. Makes 2 loaves. Bake for one hour at 350° Serve with tea and butter deliciously

*Printed on each of these beautiful tea towels are a different grandmother's recipe. Both women were from Nova Scotia and both were excellent bakers. The "Love" tea towel, however, is another story!*

**Short bread Cookies**
(or first prize at the Cookie Exchange!)

2 cups white flour

1 cup butter

½ Cup icing sugar

1 egg yolk

Dash of salt

3 or 4 caps of almond flavouring. Soften butter slightly, stir in sugar, almond flavouring, egg yolk with a Wooden spoon(!) Turn onto a floured board and knead lightly until dough begins to crack. Roll out ¼" thick and cut in to shapes. Bake at 350° until Delicately Brown (8-10 min) Store in a Cool Cookie tin.

I love the warmth of a stove-warmed kitchen; I love using my big old mixing bowl (I bought the same type my grandmother had!), I love wooden spoons for softening butter and I like wearing a printed apron and wiping my hands on thick honeycomb tea towels. I love the smells that slowly emerge, drawing people to the kitchen. And I love choosing a favorite plate and piling it high with cookies and biscuits.

In the background, the radio brightens my mood and after an hour or so of baking, my therapy is complete; with my bounty on the table, I feel as satisfied and pleased with myself as if I'd cooked for a week!

RIGHT: *Vintage, retro, country, fresh, natural— what is this look? Well, it's a little bit of all of those. Old wicker—but in sunshiny yellow with old fashioned striped cushions—pretty bouquets, coral cabinets with arts and crafts detailing, old family photos, new Haitian art and hand-printed tea towels are all combined to create a family kitchen that is both practical and personal.*

# life at home:
# handmade touches

# Cloth Laid Gently

I see –
beauty in the common place,
common action, common grace.
A cloth laid gently on the ground,
a metal cup that meets my lips
and sweet water that I sip,
I see –
milkweed stretching to the light,
yellow clovers in a crowd,
wild berries hidden in the green,
and bees so busy at their work,
that a languid dragonfly seems on holiday
I measure the grasses in their height,
count the ferns with my glance, and
note the butterfly as it alights;
this is summer, nature's feast,
and beauty is now commonplace.

# *Seeing with Your Hands*

In the conundrum that is decorating and design, I have tried to explain a few of my personal philosophies of decorating. I have discussed color and the benefits of using your walls as a canvas of color, in order to create a background for your furniture and to add an atmosphere to a room—people respond to color. I have also discussed furniture and how major pieces, such as bed, couch, table and cabinets set the tone of a room and lead you to logical choices. Natural materials such as wood, brass, cotton and glass are important to use because they complement each other in building a unified design vocabulary. I have also emphasized the importance of personal choice, and how having a personal connection to your belongings can add emotional value to your environment. Most important of all, I have discussed how letting nature into your home, through flowers, sunlight and objects that take nature as their inspiration, can add richness to your home.

As Chris says, "I've always liked things that have character and soul" and objects "where you can see the human hand that sculpted it." Behind just about everything we own there is the work of the human hand. It is almost all handmade. When I look at a quilt, I look with my hands. I feel the cotton—and my hand talks to my mind and says "natural," "cotton fields," "cotton pods." My fingers feel softness. When I touch lace edging, I feel the yarn and the delicate scalloped pattern of crochet. Crochet hooks conjure up the timeless image of women sitting in a circle and talking, as long reams of white crochet borders emerge from their needles, and slowly, piles of their white cotton yarn grow smaller.

RIGHT: *I call this watercolor painting in my bedroom "After the Party." It captures the feel of an end of a happy evening.*

I look at one of my prints and see pinks, violets, ivorys and apple greens—a riot of color, straight out of a June garden. There are hanging bleeding hearts, triumphant wigelia and peonies heavy-headed with too much sweetness. I love the pattern-painted bouquets of roses and tulips with their beautiful tapered leaves. I see a garden—many gardens—condensed into this print. I see springtime giving way to summer. I look at patchwork squares and see hand tailoring. I can feel the care and professionalism of a dedicated craftsman. It is not just a bedcover to me—not just a cotton filled quilt—it is a wonder, a handmade wonder, and I appreciate it with my eye, my hand and my mind. If you love things handmade, as we do, you will find that hand-made goods create their own decorating lexicon. They form a commonality of style that work together. The handmade has a language of its own. The hand of the craftsman always shines through.

ABOVE: *A beautiful teak cabinet from India has a border of painted ceramic tiles, each one different. There is a classic sunburst carving in the center of the cabinet door. Atop the cabinet are family photos.*

RIGHT: *Old handmade hammers, in front of the heavy cast iron panel on the foot of the bed, make the visual connection between tools and craft.*

# The Language of the Handmade

RIGHT: *Collections of
delicate handkerchiefs with
fine embroideries feature
all the relationships I love.*

LEFT: *Nothing is as useful as a simple silver dish to collect pocket change on your dresser.*

## The Language of Metal:
Fretwork, ironwork, cast, bent, rustic, twisting, enamel, silver, gold and vermeil.

## The Language of Glass:
Delicate, tracery, hand-blown, cut glass, luster and translucent.

## The Language of Wood:
Turned, moldings, glowing, patina, rich, distressed, rubbed, oiled, waxed, line, form and function.

ABOVE: *Antique silver trays, delicately etched or with a hand beaded edge serve as the perfect "hold-all" for dressers and vanity tops.*

## The Language of Art:
Personal, painterly, impressionistic, stylized, informal and naïve.

RIGHT: *I love having an elegant piece of old silver at hand to hold my pretty napkins or even the daily mail.*

## The Language of Textiles:
Stitched, pleated, tucked, ruched, flounced, embroidered, crochet, French-knots, cotton, silk, wool, woven, printed, jacquard and color—all of it.

# THE ARTIST'S WORLD

An artist's world is there to see—
a hand to guide, an eye to find,
in all the world the clarity
of nature's own sagacity.
All life's pictures duly noted,
the sweep, the curve, the arching grace,
that make one's moment commonplace,
the line, the eye that follows it,
the thinking hand that renders it.
This one moment caught in time,
by pencil, brush and studied line,
ignites a visual memory
of nature's own sweet history.

Paintings are the very essence of the handmade. They express an artist's individual outlook and unique vision. Whether tightly rendered pen and ink drawings, explosive children's watercolors filled with the confidence of the young, the formal portrait of a posed maharajah, the botanical renderings of a naturalist, or a passionate oil painting of an unknown woman whose life you love to guess at. They all have in common the presence of an artist's hand.

We love to "people" our house with these diverse points of view and artistry. Sometimes the frames are as beautiful as the paintings. Our son Lee lives in New Mexico and whenever we visit, we enjoy seeing much of the handmade products from the region. There is a wealth of talented painters to be found in New Mexico, not to mention some of the most wonderful framing we have ever seen.

It is interesting how diverse areas of the globe have become pockets of artistry: Santa Fe in the United States, Bali in Indonesia, Jaipur in India, Kashmir in northern India, Istanbul in Turkey, Key West in Florida, Haiti and Jamaica in the Caribbean. All these countries have tremendously rich art and craft traditions. They are great places for artists seeking inspiration, with so much craft collected together.

LEFT: *I can't think of anything more pleasant than sitting outside and sketching. There are always flowers, nuts or leaves from the garden as willing models.*

As you journey around my house you will see the "handmade touches" I have mentioned. A turned, wooden bowl from Quebec, a painted tray from Kashmir, a collection of hammers with heavy heads from rural Vermont, ironwork beds, and cushions with tailored scallop edges. Throughout our home, there is also an abundant collection of ironware with strong and graceful silhouettes evident in candleholders, bookstands, lamps and benches that fill each room.

Handmade objects accentuate any decorating style, even though pieces may be of diverse origin they will resonate well together. The "hand" in the handmade, the person's hand, the individual touch, all shine through.

LEFT: *This plate rail represents dishes from around my life. My son Kelly gave me the lilac design when he was eight. The large plate in the center is Dutch Colonial found in southern India. The plate on the left is Portuguese. The iron tray has designs inspired from my travels and is made for us in India.*

RIGHT: *Collections come in all shapes and sizes from inkpots to figurines to paintings, statues or old books. Chris and I enjoy our collections and the varied crafts they represent.*

BELOW: *A collection of ironware lamps and candelabra.*

# Art, Design and Craft : Handmade Beauty

As an artist, I am always supremely critical of all I do. This is natural for artists—our tribe never seems to be satisfied with any of our work! And with good reason: a color is never clean enough, a leaf never quite perfectly proportioned, a flower not correctly posed, nothing lives up to expectations! I am this way and I know other artists are, too. Despite the best intentions, rarely do the results measure up to the vision.

In design (the companion of art), we are able to remedy mistakes; we can adjust color, correct balance or tilt a downward turned flower upward. Design can improve all aspects

of one's effort so that the end result is pleasing and the desired qualities captured—the vision is maintained. Even though design is a chief collaborator of art, it cannot replace craft. Why is this so? The answer is apparent to me when I see the work of the very skilled craftsmen who make my fabric designs come alive. Without them, neither a single tablecloth could be printed nor a blouse made. Although the impetus comes from my watercolor sketches and though my inspiration may lead, drive the creation of our products, it is the many hands that complete the final printed fabrics that define our collection.

The textile printing process involves highly skilled technical artists who delicately separate amorphous, impressionistic watercolor sketches into distinct and separate color entities. Painstaking attention to detail creates the fine tracings that represent every color in a print. From these tracings, silk-screens are made. Accomplished craftsmen silk-screen our fabrics by hand. These artisans, so skilled, meticulous and practiced, have years of training. The highest level of achievement is to be called a master and these are truly master craftsmen. People look at a printed fabric and ask me how I do it? The answer of course is, "Not alone."

Hundreds, even thousands of people make what we create. The ingenuity of their work lies in the handmade element, which is so important to me, the skill of the hand, the mark of the individual—these human attributes are priceless.

I love to see the craftsmanship in objects; it adds so much to the enjoyment of them. I admire the turned wooden spindles of a chair. With my hand, I feel the smoothness of the wood and I imagine the sanding, polishing and rubbing that must have taken place. I appraise the rich color of the wood, the grain and how it follows the rounded shape of the turned wood. I see not just the wood itself, but also the colored stains, developed from a lifetime's testing, learning and understanding of how to enrich and enliven wood, so that it glows like a jewel. I look at this beautiful handmade chair and I think, *nature is respected—this is a beautiful thing.* My handmade chair is as much about the history of craftsmanship as it is about pride in one's labor and art. It glows!

RIGHT: *Handmade details abound in this scene. A fine enamel box, a hand tooled brass vase and an old bedside commode represent craft at its finest. The scalloped-edging of the quilt and the hand-printed cushions say "handmade textiles."*

BELOW: *This little teapot is based on wood violets of early spring.*

I love ironware. My house and workspaces are full of it. I love its versatility and the way metal can be twisted and turned and shaped to create beautiful silhouettes. A dark bird perched on a vine becomes the fence of a naturalist's dream; heavy, iron lanterns with cut-glass panels provide pools of candlelight on a summers night; an iron hook, shaped like a leaf of the forest, holds a pretty dressing gown. It is truly a wonderfully expressive metal, and the skill of the craftsmen is there to be admired in every piece. I particularly love the way ironware can meet the demands of both form and function.

We have a wonderful iron fence surrounding our Montreal office, which overlooks the Lachine Canal. It is an historic industrial area, and in choosing to build our offices there, we

LEFT: *This bed is truly a naturalists fantasy! Imagine an afternoon nap in the shade of an old oak tree with bouquets of flowers blooming all around. We have made our outdoor bedroom just as special as a real guest room, with an iron table full of favorite books, a cotton carpet for the feet and extra blankets at the foot of the bed for when the summer sun goes down. From trailing leaves on the crisp white sheets and vibrant floral sprays on a field of cadmium yellow this fine Matalasse quilt hums with handmade action!*

made an effort keep to the period and architectural style of the neighborhood. The ironwork fence, which we commissioned, not only fit our design criteria as a delightful frame around our new building, but it also created a visual link with the historic district's industrial past. Industry aside, we couldn't resist adding some playful motifs to our fence. Blackbirds wrought in rich black iron sit atop the railings—visiting fat brown sparrows have found this to be the perfect seat for them too! From our lunchroom we appreciate their antics on the fence. In our New Delhi offices we have a canvas canopy framed by the same bird and vine iron design—I do believe in making the most of a good idea! On a hot summer day, bird after bird first perches on the canopy's ironware bird, then flies down for a long drink and dips in the birdbath below. One day, we put out some papaya and watched as our crows tore chunks off, soaked them in the water, paused, picked the papaya up

again, threw back their throats and gulped down the chunks, with what looked like total bliss. The birds of Delhi and Montreal seem to be attracted to the same sense of style in fences!

Some people admire the latest electronic invention: the newest computer, the finest television, or a well-made car. While I, too, see the value in these things and the benefits of good design and improved use, what I truly love and respect are handmade things. The embroidered rose, the printed cloth, the brass vase, the finely painted box—these are the items that Chris and I admire. We enjoy being in a business that allows for the continuity of skills that are often centuries old. We love drawing attention to the time-honored aesthetic of the handmade and breathing new life into old crafts. We appreciate the skilled craftsmen and women who interpret our designs and ideas and imbue our efforts with the richness of their talents. I guess you could say that we just love everything handmade!

LEFT: *A variety of cushion shapes can add depth to a bedroom presentation. Note the round "Puffetta" and the delicately shirred "Bon-Bon" cushion.*

BELOW: *Sun filtered through glass creates delightful shadows in this gentle setting. An organdy tablecloth with appliquéd leaves is offset by our vintage inspired vineyard glassware.*

# entertaining with
# the seasons

# The Privilege of Guests

Ahh — the privilege of guests — the arrival of company,

the anticipation of a party,

three birthday cakes, finding candles,

counting silver, striking matches,

peeling, stirring, apron wearing,

thinking, tasting, —

tablecloth in final pressing,

candies scattered out in bowls.

Add the lipstick, check the mirror, tie the hair,

mmm…mmm —

smell the baking?  what about music?

I think they're coming —

I can hear them there's the bell —

yes — it's them!

# Something for Everyone

I love a party. I love attending them and I enjoy having them. I like small intimate ones with just a couple, I love garden parties with a crowd, I love busy cocktails with lots of chat and wedding receptions full of emotion. But of all the different kinds of parties, my favorite ones are family parties, parties with my three sons. As my mother-in-law, Mary Cornell, has said many a time, "April, we have shared many birthday cakes together! And each one has been wonderful." I like to go a little overboard in the cake department and make sure everyone has something they like: one all chocolate for the purists, one vanilla because the sprinkles show well on it and one vanilla with chocolate icing for the undecided. Our summer parties are usually outdoors, taking advantage of the garden. Our middle son Lee's birthday is in May and by then we are generally aching for the first barbecue and outdoor activity by the time the special day arrives. Plates of steaks, burgers piled high, frosty beers in ice buckets, Coca-Colas, three cakes, gifts with funny wrappings and a crowd of his friends are all part of Lee's birthday and the start of summer in our family.

## The Well-Dressed Table

Table settings can really be as elaborate as you want them to be—it depends on taste and the occasion. For the every day, I love a simple table with a bright cloth and a bouquet of flowers—the cloth laid in a diamond pattern, so corners of the wooden table show. This is my general welcoming set-up all through the year. Now, what about more specific occasions?

Breakfast for two, even a simple breakfast for two, is worth the effort. I usually put two mats (printed fabric placemats) on a wooden table and then match them up with two napkins in a solid color. The solid color napkins should match one of the colors of the multi-hued place-mat, or, use a check pattern that can be color-coordinated with the table mats. A check or a polka-dot pattern makes the setting more casual and a little more retro in feel. The fifties were known for checks and plaids and when I use a check with a print, I feel it pulls a little fifties style into a room. This is a style that has a lot of nostalgia to it. Marry it up with a painterly print and it becomes much more than the fifties ever were. Polka-dots will do the same, but in an even more lighthearted way. The centerpiece of the

LEFT: *Flowers and vases that reflect the same colors as the tablecloth are perfect accessories. A bold mix of different colors enhances a table setting outdoors.*

BELOW: *A crisply starched white tea cloth is the perfect foil for adding color. A pink pitcher, pastel teacakes and our "Fraise" dishes provide the setting for a tea party in the garden.*

breakfast table should be a pretty container to hold the toast or scones. It could be a basket with a printed or check napkin lining or a cake stand that makes an event of two bagels and a bun! This vertical element lifts the scene up a little, just as candles do, and adds to the elegance of presentation. Morning, don't you love it? A couple of attractive glasses for juice, a teapot and two cups will be all you need for this simple breakfast, but I am careful not to minimize my effort by putting milk cartons

RIGHT: *A plaid tablecloth, with warm autumn colors, kitchen chairs pulled outside, crockery with a pattern of apples or a warm pie—these simple ingredients speak to the season approaching fall, and add to the enjoyment of a late afternoon in September.*

and plastic containers on the table. I like to use a little pitcher of milk for the tea or coffee. The butter is always in a dish too. I use an antique one from my grandmother—there's the sense of decorating history being handed down, and moving forward. Really, these are such small details, but they add a lot of grace to a table.

Another simple setting I like is a small white lace runner in the middle of the table with two printed mats, and maybe two lace napkins to match. The crisp whiteness of a piece of vintage lace (or a good imitation) displays beautifully against wood. A colored ceramic vase will contrast nicely with the white table runner and your flowers can pick up colors from the placemats. Mixing patterns with plaids is not as complicated as it may seem. I stick to a color palette, unless I am feeling particularly bold, and everything matches that way. A plaid cloth layered over a print, the addition of printed napkins,

OPPOSITE: *Red, white and blue carries the day for a summer picnic. Blueberries and watermelon make the perfect color choice for fruits.*

LEFT: *I love enamel-ware—the fact that it is not disposable and is virtually indestructible are two of its best features. I like the thought that we will still be using it for picnics years from now.*

BELOW: *A trio of cushions provides a place to put your head for that coveted afternoon nap on a summer day.*

or a mix of alternating printed and solid napkins will all work together if the colors are similar. Remember, most prints have golds or greens or red tones in them, so these are easy accents to play up. I am not a stickler for an exact match. It seldom satisfies completely, and you can frustrate yourself over it, and really miss the point of joyful entertaining. I step back and look at a table and see if it feels balanced. Sometimes, something I thought would work together doesn't quite come off, and I find I need to add a third ingredient to balance the color. Usually it means matching the color from the print in a stronger way.

## Bistro Style

If you are having a party where you can use a few tables, it is fun to put one palette together and then mix it up on the other tables. On one table could be plaid, on another a floral print

and on a third a jacquard. As long as the same colors are threading their way through all of the tables, the total look will be unified. In fact, you should feel a positive hum from the room! Call this "Bistro Style," make it jazzy and use it in the evening with tea lights and great music. Alternatively, call it "Garden Party Style" and make it romantic and fresh with flowers and fresh fruit.

A few years ago we held a wedding in our garden for a dear friend. We used just such a strategy for decorating the tables. We didn't have enough of any single cloth, but we had an

array of cloths in a variety of yellows. From fine organdies on the head table, to crisp cotton prints and yellow jacquards, we created a presence of color that felt like a sunny fairyland. There were ivory undercloths to set off the toppers, which added a foundation to the décor. The napkins were different shades of yellow—from lemon to butter to gold. The tables were then topped with flats of pink impatience, adding an extra highlight, and an element of surprise to the settings. The bride shone in a soft yellow tulle dress, and her teenage entourage, twenty-four year old bridesmaids and groomsmen made an avenue of youthful excitement for her and her kilted groom to walk through.

RIGHT: *A staging table in the background, covered in Tuscan lace, makes a useful work area while adding to the elegance of this outdoor scene. The cushions are in the same colors as the printed cloth but each is a different pattern. The colors in this setting could also work indoors for a party in autumn or winter.*

## Dinner Party

For a dinner party, if serving dishes are plentiful and glasses are filling the table, I would keep the setting simple. I like to select a tablecloth that matches the color of my dishes. I use solid color dishes for my place settings; our prints are so multi-colored that there is not much of a problem finding a match. I use matching napkins, or contrasting solid ones to complete the look. With wine decanters, casserole dishes and platters of food, there isn't much room for additional décor—I let the food take center stage. Don't forget the candles, though. They help bring the conversation up to eye level.

## Picnic Party

Throw a blanket on the ground, add some plump pillows for seating, bowls of chunky watermelon, maybe some spiced chicken and a summer picnic unfolds. A simple theme can add an activity to a party, making it memorable. A painting theme is fun and an easy choice for a picnic. Have on hand a couple of sketchbooks, watercolors for the artists and a box of crayons so everyone can join in and give a theme to a summer day. And what a way to notice and note nature in its summer best— dragonflies taking flight and wildflowers pushing up from the grass.

## Garden Party.

A garden party can speak to many occasions, but is in itself an event. It is difficult to go wrong with a garden party. So much of the decorating is already done! A table setting outdoors should take advantage of a summer afternoon in the splendor of a lush garden. Don't be afraid to experiment with different colors to enhance your table setting. A pretty blue printed cloth filled with a pattern of summer roses can be accented with pink dishes or a palette of pink napkins. Use flowers and vases as accessories that reflect the same colors as the tablecloth. A crisply starched white tea cloth on top is the perfect foil for adding color. A pink pitcher, pastel teacakes and our "Fraise" dishes

BELOW: *Half the fun is getting ready for the party! Tossing a tablecloth can add a few relaxing laughs to the preparations of the day.*

LEFT: *A bouquet of Bittersweet picks up the colors in the "Conservatory" tablecloth.*

provide the perfect setting for a tea party in the beautiful garden.

There are no set formulas, especially when entertaining outdoors. A garden party could also have a series of tables, each dressed slightly differently to add visual interest. Use old purchases with new but maintain a balance in order to carry it off successfully.

Keep the mood delicate and light; outdoor table settings are perfect for a bridal shower, an afternoon with female friends or an old fashioned strawberry social.

## Lunch Party

As long as it is not too chilly, outdoor entertaining can be stretched through the fall. The setting for a lunch party could easily move into fall, or serve for a southern Christmas occasion. Burgundy tones with hints of red in the print, shimmering lusterware and accents of purple wine-colored dishes offset with white lace cloth on the serving table and make an outdoor party formal enough for very special events. The wine and red colors also provide flexibility and contribute to the ability to move table settings forward to Christmas and indoors for fall holidays. The chair cushions are matching in color but not design, which adds a seemingly spontaneous and personal touch to an elegant presentation.

*Easter*

As little girls, my two sisters and I always received a new outfit for Easter, right down to the shoes and bonnet. Many people still want to dress up in new outfits and celebrate the approach of spring. I know I do. When Easter falls in March, it is still very cold in Vermont but I always look forward to our local spring flower show (indoors, of course) to fill the house full of daffodils and hyacinths, tulips and pussy willows. Every gardener heaves a sigh of anticipatory happiness as lengthening days signal that the earth is awakening again.

Easter morning ranks right up there with Halloween as a special day for children. We have always hidden chocolate all over the downstairs of our home for Easter.

In vases, under cushions, on top of paintings—sometimes an egg shows up months later, hidden far too well to be found. To our delight, we provided the tablecloths at the White House Easter Egg Roll for three years running. An egg roll—now, that sounds like fun.

LEFT: *In this Easter scene, our antique spice box holds a mix of fresh brown eggs and painted ones. The "Bleached Blue" Nova Scotia palette on the tablecloth and cushions is a permanent spring favorite of ours. On the benches, old and new patterns of cushions in a similar blue palette mix easily together.*

# *Thanksgiving*

LEFT: *Dried autumn hydrangeas and roses are reflected in the mirror of this old, British colonial cabinet from India. I like the way the mirror reflects the room, adding another scene to the field of view.*

"Thanksgiving" is such a wonderful word. It keeps us mindful of what there is to be thankful for, particularly the bounty of the earth in all its autumnal plenitude. It also harks back to the tradition in North America of harvest and storing for winter ahead.

In Canada, Thanksgiving is celebrated in early October. We have many family memories of turkey cooked in our unheated chalet with everyone clustered near the stove keeping warm from the steam of cooking vegetables.

These days we celebrate Thanksgiving in November, but often in the tropics, where we do not shiver but enjoy the warm trade winds, with a turkey on the beach and under the stars.

RIGHT: *The harvest season calls for harvest colors. Pumpkins decorate the borders of these plaid mats and napkins with large pumpkins on them make a strong contrast to the plaid.*

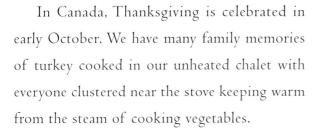

LEFT: *Chris and I strategize on the table décor before a dinner party.*

RIGHT: *A harvest table is readied for the family.*

Between Canadian and American Thanksgiving lies one of my favorite holidays—Halloween! When our children were small (and all children seem to grow up slowly where Halloween is concerned), we celebrated Halloween with fervor. We were lucky to live on a very busy street with many trick or treaters— no matter how much candy we anticipated we always seemed to run short! Our own children swarmed the street with a gang of friends and we manned the door. A home-made macaroni meal became the tra-ditional fare of the evening and in between

# Give Thanks

Give thanks

for your food.

Give thanks

for the day.

Give thanks to each other

and those far away.

It is Thanksgiving.

Give thanks today.

ringing doorbells the adults feasted buffet style. By eight o'clock only school apples were left to give out. We turned off the lights and joined in the counting (and selecting) of candy.

This is a great holiday to make a fuss about. Children love it and it creates lasting memories for them. As adults, it is fun to be observers of the fun and delight of children, rather than orchestrating it. And one doesn't need to have children to enjoy giving out candy. A simple buffet with family friendly food, a pumpkin centerpiece on harvest cloth, and a jack-o-lantern on the steps are all that are required.

BELOW: *One of the artworks for our harvest design is shown below. The technical separation of colors can be seen through the numbering. On the left is the finished product—cushions and tablecloths.*

LEFT: *Pheasants, quail and ruffed grouse decorate these cushions. This design was conceived during a very rainy holiday in the Laurentian mountains where I was lucky enough to spot a scurrying ruffed grouse trying to get out of the rain.*

# Christmas

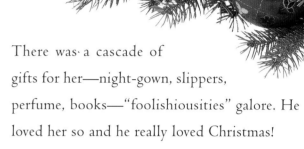

Generosity was my father's middle name and Christmas to me is always a tribute to his love of Christmas and sheer delight in giving. Though some say Christmas is too commercial and it is not all about gifts, in our home there is still an amplitude of presents and a joy in the season.

My mother loves to tell the story of her first Christmas with my father. They were newly-weds living in Halifax, while my father was completing his degree. My mother was expecting and expectant of their first Christmas together. She carefully prepared a tiny tabletop tree and placed her one beautifully wrapped gift beneath it. Christmas morning arrived and my father brought his family traditions and enthusiasm for his new wife to the morning.

LEFT: *Think of an intimate moment, perhaps it is breakfast, when you sit down, and enjoy the peace of the day. A pretty silver rim teacup and a cheery red placemat add elegance. The cedar sprig adds seasonal spirit.*

BELOW: *Before the house fills with family and friends, I like to take time to exchange a gift with my husband. We have our tea and a traditional breakfast while sitting at a table dressed with favorite treasures.*

There was a cascade of gifts for her—night-gown, slippers, perfume, books—"foolishiousities" galore. He loved her so and he really loved Christmas!

Gift giving is very personal and it can go both ways. I say express yourself if you love giving gifts—enjoy yourself and do it as often as you can. If you prefer to express yourself with a single thoughtfully chosen present then do just that. The pleasure, truly, is as much for the giver as it is for the receiver.

Christmas entertaining really starts for our family in New Delhi. Chris and I and our oldest son Cameron make a point of being in India for *Divali* (the "Festival of Lights" celebrates the symbolic triumph of good over evil). We celebrate the Festival of Lights with our Indian staff. We have over four hundred and fifty employees in India and I think they all like to have a good time! People turn up in their absolute finest for parties. The women are gorgeous in silk saris—turquoise, wines, golds, and sophisticated blacks—whatever the latest trend;

it is displayed in all its "splendiousity" at *Divali* time. Men may wear traditional silk *kameez* and *churidar*, or western business suits.

*Divali* is a time to go all out. Chris, Cameron and I join in the fun and shop for new outfits each year. There is nothing more elegant than a good-looking guy in a classic Nehru-style outfit, trust me! At *Divali* time a traditional exchange of sweets make the days leading up to *Divali* full of surprises. Elaborately and creatively presented sweets arrive continually and are shared by all.

A family get together is held and all those who are not in town are present by telephone. For a traveling mom and, indeed, family, I say

BELOW: *Tea time is made special with hand-painted mugs and a pretty embroidered tea cozy. An old mirror turned into a tray keeps the whole scene novel.*

thank you for the telephone. It is an important tool that helps include everyone in special events. Cards come in from grandparents—they never miss a birthday! And the dishes on the table are a mix of vegetarian and "meatatarian." As my son Kelly used to say, "I'm not a vegetarian, I don't eat vegetables!" Following Cameron's birthday we rush into company parties in both Montreal and Vermont. Venues change from year to year from our company kitchen, to city clubs, black box theatres and local golf courses. Dressing up is *de rigueur*. It is amazing how people can "lay on the look" and some are quite unrecognizable.

The Christmas tree is now up at home; the wreaths are on the doors, the red cloth on the kitchen table, "brocade luxiouriosity" in the dining room and shortbread baking trial batches start. Cards are written—thank goodness for once a year catching up! Packages are boxed up and sent to many family members far away and a mass of Christmas lights twinkle outside. We've always had lights outside, but recently, I've felt it even more important to show a proud "face" street side. It is the old light in the window idea—and I want to let it shine! Perhaps my experiences of so many Festival of Light celebrations in India have influenced me too. Christmas morning can be anywhere—Vermont, the Caribbean, Montreal, or the Far East, wherever I am, I still make a breakfast that just keeps on coming as people arrive and gifts are opened. Hot coffee, fragrant tea and hot chocolate provide a warm drink for everyone to linger over.

Occasions are very memorable (and moving). The symbolic elements—food, décor, color— are all that's required to bring the holidays to life in different settings. Immigrants the world over have carried traditions by land and sea to new countries. It is not the place but the purpose that is important. New customs should join with old to keep tradition meaningful and light hearted. People should enjoy the celebration, feel soothed by the symbolic aspects and cheered by the sense of creating.

BELOW: *At Christmas I like to hand-paint special cards for my family and friends to let them know they are in my thoughts.*

# Traditional Christmas or "Killer" Eggnog

*18 eggs*

*2 cups extra fine granulated sugar*

*4 cups Bourbon (optional)*

*1 cup Cognac*

*1 teaspoon vanilla*

*4 cups light cream (or table cream)*

*6 cups heavy cream*

*grated nutmeg*

SERVES 24

1) Separate eggs, placing yolks in a large bowl, and whites in a second large bowl.

2) Add sugar to the egg yolks, beat until fluffy. Stir in Bourbon, Cognac, vanilla and light cream. Chill several hours or until very cold.

3) Beat egg whites until they stand in peaks. Beat heavy cream until stiff in a large bowl. Fold beaten egg whites and whipped cream into egg yolk mixture. Pour into a very large bowl. Sprinkle with grated nutmeg.

4) Ladle into punch cups.

OPPOSITE: *A pretty patchwork tablecloth sets the mood. I like to put out extra cushions on my chairs to let people know they can make themselves comfortable and sit a while.*

*Chapter Six*

# making the everyday special

## Peaceful Day

I start my day with a peaceful
moment - a cup of coffee with my
husband. We share the paper, sniff
the local news and look forward to the
day ahead.

My beautiful cup warms my hand,
Chris sinks into our kitchen armchair
there are smells of potent coffee and
fragrant tea. It is a moment - a peaceful
moment for all eternity.

It is these peaceful moments -
these simple pleasures, these sublime
times of awesome understated beauty -
that nourish us, encourage us, replenish
us and help us flourish.

# Peaceful Moments

Chris and I have spent our careers in the retail world; our daily schedule is a reflection of this world. At retail end, the opening of shops starts late, so we do have the luxury of getting off to a late start. What this meant for our family when the children were young, was our mornings weren't rushed, we had time to make lunches, have breakfast and get the children to school before getting ready ourselves. These late timings have formed the framework of our day. A cup of coffee shared, news reviewed and the day's planning discussed in quiet relaxation before we, too, must get up and go. These moments are important—a lifetime of them adds real value to your health and to your relationships. These moments are what I call "everyday occasions." In this Chapter, you will see settings that are simple, yet emphasize the point of enjoying the moment—the importance of making small occasions out of the everyday.

Having a garden is wonderful and I thank the lucky day we found our home with its wonderful garden in downtown Burlington, Vermont. Gracious old trees include a rare Douglas fir, a full hemlock hedge, a huge old oak, a wonderfully mature maple and mysterious tamarack. Add to this rambles of raspberry and blackberries, carpets of wild strawberry, trilli-

*BELOW: What a treat it is to pick a bouquet on a September afternoon.*

ums in the early spring, lily of the valley near the fence and delicate ferns. Imagine all of this in the middle of Vermont's largest city! It certainly was a wonderful surprise for Chris and I moving from downtown Montreal ten years ago. It is one of the distinct advantages of living in a small town with old, well-maintained homes. We have added many features to the garden over the years: a pond (excellent for the birds' needs year round), a drying shed and a bulb border with a thousand springtime tulips. Rose bushes seem to thrive and cascade over the fieldstone wall. I love planting a variety of nasturtiums every season. The golds, oranges,

LEFT: *Amid the bramble and buried in the greenery, a comfortable chair with book, coffee and binoculars speaks of a moment taken to appreciate nature in its transitory beauty.*

BELOW: *Sometimes a chair just calls out to the sitter, "Pick up a book and put your feet up, this chair is waiting for you."*

*Plants of the Stumpery*

Asarum europaeum — European Ginger
Athyrium 'Brandford Rambler'
Athyrium filix — femina 'Vernoniae Cristata' — Crested Lady Fern
Athyrium niponicum 'Pictum' — Japanese Painted Fern
Geranium robertianum — Herb Robert
Heuchera 'Chocolate Ruffles' — Chocolate Ruffles Coral Bells
Humulus lupulus 'Aurea' — Golden Hope Vine
Hydrangea anomala subsp. petiolaris — Climbing Hydrangea
Lamium maculatum 'Checkers' — Dead Nettle
Lilium martagon — Turk's Cap Lily
Rhus typhina — Staghorn Sumac
Rubus 'Royalty' — Purple Raspberry
Viola labradorica — Labrador Violet

rusts and reds of the beautiful rounded leaves sprawl across the patio, well into October.

I use my garden as a reference library for leaf and flower shapes, nuts and berries, but mostly we use it for relaxing and unwinding. Collecting an armful of flowers is a real treat on a Saturday morning—a special occasion in itself. It causes me to wander around my garden examining leaves and stems and flowers, deciding

which to pick and which to leave. This is a truly luxurious moment. The cut flowers go in a glass pitcher or a pretty ceramic vase and brighten the kitchen for the next few days. This brings nature indoors and emphasizes the special quality of the humble kitchen table.

A chair tucked into a wooded area is an opportunity to tuck away a little time in silent contemplation. While sitting outdoors during the summer, completely hidden in the trees, I saw a little bird hopping nearby in the dogwood bush—a newcomer to the garden. Quietly, I watched this small summer wren, a new sighting for my backyard diary. Also in our backyard is a stump, the solitary remnant of a majestic Douglas fir that toppled during an ice storm. It came down with a sharp crack, its great length crashing in a diagonal across the lawn. A single slate tile was knocked off the roof of the garage—the broken tile exposed a hole, which became a nesting spot for a family of European Starlings. Their chuckling, whistling and confounding calls make me look up every time I leave the house. The remaining stump has become a stumpery now planted with a garden of delicate ferns, European ginger, coral bells, staghorn sumacs, purple raspberry and

LEFT: *The garden birds love to bathe in our pond. Pigeons, cardinals, cedar waxwings and many others line up and take turns preening and playing in the water.*

the delicate and beautiful Turk's cap lily. It is also home to our friendly and famous groundhog who likes the wild strawberries right outside her door. Luckily, she has held back on eating the ferns! Seeing this beautiful brown beast lumber out with her new batch of babies every spring gives the whole family a laugh. Groundhogs like to search for new shoots, and we hope we have planted enough both for our taste and hers! Many curse her, but I enjoy a chuckle every time I spot her. The chopped wood of the eighty-year-old fir, downed in the storm, burned brightly for the next two winters. Nature, once again, showed a surprising outcome for a downed tree.

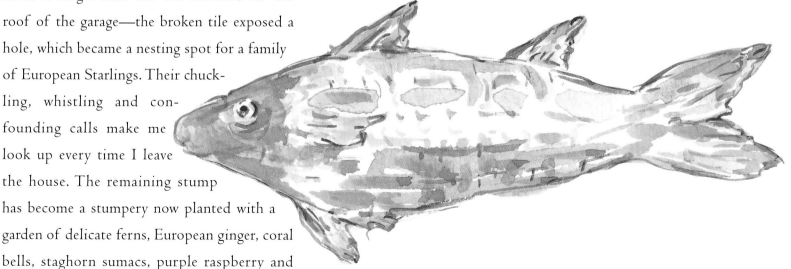

There is something so nostalgic about a wooden swing. I don't know if it is an old-fashioned image of lovers rocking gently together, the soft creak of the swing filling the air of a summer night, or perhaps it is the thought of children at wild play enjoying its simple back and forth mechanics.

Whatever the reason, people do love a swing! We have a big wooden swing in our garden. Decorated with some thick cushions, it is a perfect place to sit for a private chat, or a solitary read. I have planted the area around the swing with day lilies, bee balm and cone flowers. It is a haven for butterflies and bees. A two-year-old wisteria climbs the frame. We are waiting for its first blooms.

In the back of the yard, an old oak tree supports a rope swing. Playing on the swing—whether pushing or being pushed—is an old-fashioned activity that hasn't lost its appeal. One beautiful July day, when we hosted a friend's wedding, we decorated this rope swing with garlands of flowers and little girl after little girl had her picture taken.

*Flowers of the Swing*

Hermerocallis 'Patricia Fay' — Patricia Far Daylily

Lonicera x heckrottii — Goldflame Honeysuckle

Monarda 'Blaustrumpf' — Blue Stocking Beebalm

Nepeta 'Walkers Low' — Walker's Low Catmint

Verbena bonariensis — Purpletop Vervain

Wisteria macrostachys 'Aunt Dee' — Aunt Dee Kenucky Wisteria

# Observing the Everyday

I don't like to be without a notebook or a pencil, and no, the notebook is not full of appointments, or "to do lists"—(in fact, some would suggest I am woefully unorganized). It is a notebook to record sightings and observations, to write down ideas, to draw and paint flowers, birds, leaves, to note colors as I travel and to paint ideas for future references. I use these notebooks in my work. An idea may come to life immediately, or it may lie quietly for several years, until something completes the thought and its usefulness is shown. I have a lot of these notebooks around. I'm quite good at misplacing things—but I never throw them out. Eventually they all come into use. The noting of daily events, such as a flock of cedar waxwings spotted drinking in the pond, pigeons strutting like proud matrons over the lawn, the first blooms of beautiful pink peonies, the heavy head of scented lilacs, brave poppies in a June breeze, strawberries underfoot, voices of children heard playing next door, apple blossoms blanketing the grass—all these scenes of nature are kept for future contemplation, information and inspiration in my notebook.

My favorite Windsor & Newton paint box travels with me everywhere! A bowl of walnuts from the Calgary farmers' market, once they

BELOW: *Chris and I enjoy a glass of wine together at the restful end of a busy day.*

LEFT: *Blue place mat, yellow plate, brown egg and the filter of a morning sun; this small "tableau" creates an instant message of peacefulness and beauty. This is such a simple presentation, yet so effective in creating beauty in the everyday.*

wrinkle up, are future candidates for painting. On many transatlantic flights I have painted things that inspire me during recent European visits. Pretty vessels hold the brushes so that the act of painting is itself a still life and an artistic moment, an added value to my efforts. It is also an everyday occasion. A few years ago, I started to describe myself as an artist. I didn't really mean to say, "Hey, I'm a painter." What I meant to say was that I see the world through an artist's eye. I see the form and line of life, in an appreciative way. My hand wants to hold a pencil. My being wants to be surrounded by beauty. Nature calls and thrills me. My eyes

LEFT: *The end of day sunlight filters through this decanter and glasses set on a brass tray. They hold a promise of a special evening to come.*

Cocktails 7pm tonight — Please come.

April and Chris

sometimes hurt from looking, staring, thinking and drinking in all of life, seeing what is all around me.

In the ordinary, one sees the extraordinary—the perfect oval of a brown egg, the fine complexity of a fern, light falling on a chair, the pouring of a red wine in a shaped glass, the red and golden colors of my son's hair, the blue of his eyes, the fresh color of his freckled skin, the mahogany tones of his friend's complexion or the tangled auburn curls of my friend's hair. There is so much to see—so much to enjoy. That is what being an artist means to me. It is not about painting or drawing, though I love to do that. It is about seeing, and that is how I think about my customers, too—as artists, other people out there having a good look at the surrounding world.

I hope you have enjoyed the tour around our home. I hope that you feel comfortable with my decorating ideas and with my thoughts. May your everyday be special.

# Sources

## April Cornell Store List - U.S.

The Summit
310 Summit Blvd.
Birmingham, AL 35243
205-970-1660

Kierland Commons
15054 N. Scottsdale Road
Scottsdale, AZ 85254
480-607-7790

1774 Fourth Street
Berkeley, CA 94710
510-527-0715

The Village at Corte Madera
1628 Redwood Highway
Corte Madera, CA 94925
415-924-5880

1000 Prospect Street
La Jolla, CA 92037
858-454-1980

Fashion Island
1111 Newport Center Drive
Newport Beach, CA 92660
949-721-9061

The Gardens on El Paseo
Palm Desert, CA 92260
60-341-8372

Paseo Colorado
340 East Colorado Blvd.
Pasadena, CA 91101
626-440-7253

Arden Fair Mall
1689 Arden Way
Sacramento, CA 95815
916-925-5940

Fashion Valley
7007 Friars Road
San Diego, CA 92108
619-298-8482

Paseo Nuevo
301 Paseo Nuevo
Santa Barbara, CA 93101
805-899-4689

Valley Fair Shopping Center
2855 Stevens Creek
Santa Clara, CA 95050
408-261-9970

1180 Broadway Plaza
Walnut Creek, CA 94596
925-939-2437

1123 Pearl Street
Boulder, CO 80302
303-442-3723

1 West Flat Iron Circle
Broomfield, CO 80021
303-439-2179

Cherry Creek Shopping Center
3000 E. First Ave.
Denver, CO 80206
303-316-9898

Danbury Fair Mall
7 Backus Ave.
Danbury, CT 06811
203-791-1137

West Farms Mall
406 West Farms Mall
Farmington, CT 06032
860-521-1923

92 Greenwich Ave.
Greenwich, CT 06830
203-661-3563

3278 M. Street NW
Washington, DC 20007
202-625-7887

The Falls
8888 SW 136th
Miami, FL 33176
305-254-2204

The Gardens of the
Palm Beaches
3101 PGA Blvd.
Palm Beach, FL 33410
561-625-6979

Old Hyde Park Village
800 S. Village Circle
Old Hyde Park
Tampa, FL 33606
813-251-3019

Lenox Mall
3393 Peachtree Road NE
Atlanta, GA 30326
404-812-1722

Perimeter Mall
4400 Ashford Dunwoody Road
Atlanta, GA 30346
770-671-0722

The Forum
5155 Peachtree Parkway
Norcross, GA 30092
770-447-8021

Deer Park Town Center
20530 N. Rand Road
Deer Park, IL 60010
847-540-5909

2228 Northbrook Court
Northbrook, IL 60062
847-564-8570

Oakbrook Mall
417 Oakbrook Mall
Oakbrook, IL 60523
630-574-3066

Keystone at the Crossing
8702 Keystone Crossing
Indianapolis, IN 46240
317-569-9289

Faneuil Hall Marketplace
6 North Marketplace Building
Boston, MA 02109
617-248-0280

43 Brattle Street
Cambridge, MA 02138
617-661-8910

The Mall at Chestnut Hill
199 Boylston Street
Chestnut Hill
Newton, MA 02467
617-965-1126

Wrentham Village
Premium Outlets
One Premium Outlets Blvd.
Wrentham, MA 02093
508-384-9538

16 Marketplace
Annapolis, MD 21401
410-263-4532

Harborplace - The Gallery
200 East Pratt Street
Baltimore, MD 21202
410-234-0050

The Mall in Columbia
10300 Little Patuxent Parkway
Columbia, MD 21044
410-730-9007

Prime Outlets Hagerstown
835 Prime Outlets Blvd.
Hagerstown, MD 21740
301-790-1313

Towson Town Center
825 Dulaney Valley Road
Towson, MD 21204
410-823-0833

Somerset Collection
2800 W. Big Beaver Road
Troy, MI 48084
248-816-9660

The Galleria
3565 Galleria
Edina, MN 55435
952-836-0830

Country Club Plaza
415 Nichols Road
Kansas City, MO 64112
816-960-0333

1166 St. Louis Galleria
St. Louis, MO 63117
314-725-0120

Crabtree Valley Mall
4325 Glenwood Ave.
Raleigh, NC 27612
919-781-7817

13 Settler's Green
North Conway, NH 03860
603-356-0820

Bridgewater Commons Mall
400 Common Way
Bridgewater, NJ 08807
908-218-9699

51 Palmer Square West
Princeton, NJ 08542
609-921-3559

The Mall at Short Hills
1200 Morris Turnpike
Short Hills, NJ 07078
973-258-0660

The Grove at Shrewsbury
567 Route 35
Shrewsbury, NJ 07702
732-758-0066

487 Columbus Ave.
New York, NY 10024
212-799-4342

Kenwood Town Center
7875 Montgomery Road
Cincinnati, OH 45236
513-936-8819

Pioneer Place
340 SW Morrison Street
Portland, OR 97204
503-222-2171

Suburban Square
Shopping Center
29 On the Square
Ardmore, PA 19003
610-642-9540

King of Prussia Mall
Court of King of Prussia
King of Prussia, PA 19406
610-265-0317

The Shops at Liberty Place
1625 Chestnut Street
Philadelphia, PA 19103
215-981-0350

244 King Street
Charleston, SC 29401
843-805-7000

Greenville Mall
1025 Woodruff Road
Greenville, SC 29607
864-234-9667

Oak Court
4465 Poplar Ave.
Memphis, TN 38117
901-767-9110

Arboretum
10000 Research Blvd
Austin, TX 78759
512-345-9908

North Park Center
Dallas, TX 75225
214-750-8338

River Oaks
2004 West Gray
Houston, TX 77019
713-520-0426

Highland Village
4024 Westheimer Road
Houston, TX 77027
713-599-1387

The Shops at Willow Bend
6121 West Park
Plano, TX 75093
972-202-5536

Fashion Center
at Pentagon City
1100 S. Hayes
Arlington, VA 22202
703-415-2290

Tysons Corner Center
8038L Tysons Corner Center
McLean, VA 22102
703-448-6972

MacArthur Place
300 Monticello Ave.
Norfolk, VA 23510
757-625-5804

Church Street Marketplace
87 Church Street
Burlington, VT 05401
802-862-8211

215 Bellevue Square
Bellevue, WA 98004
425-455-9818

Westlake Center
400 Pine Street
Seattle, WA 98101
206-749-9658

# La Cache Store List ~ Canada

Cascade Plaza
317 Banff Ave.
Banff, AB
T1L 1B7
403-760-3974

228 8th Ave. SW
Calgary, AB
T2P 1B5
403-263-5545

South Center Mall
100 Anderson Road SE
Calgary, AB
T2J 3V1
403-271-3536

111 Street & 51 Street Ave.
Edmonton, AB
T6H 4M6
780-437-9406

West Edmonton Mall
8770 170th Street
Edmonton, AB
T5T 4M2
780-481-2038

2956 Granville Street
Vancouver, BC
V6H 3J7
604-731-8343

Victoria Eaton Centre
1150 Douglas Street
Victoria, BC
V8W 3M9
250-384-6343

Park Royal North
Shopping Centre
West Vancouver, BC
V7T 1H9
604-926-3250

5657 Spring Garden Road
Halifax, NS
B3J 3R4
902-423-1844

Sherway Gardens
25 the West Mall
Etobicoke, ON
M9C 1B8
416-621-7061

2 King Street
Hamilton, ON
L8P 1A1
905-528-3270

208 Princess Street
Kingston, ON
K7L 1B2
613-544-0905

The White Oaks Mall
1105 Wellington Road
London, ON
N6E 1V4
519-680-7412

763 Bank Street
Ottawa, ON
K1S 3V3
613-233-0412

2264 Bloor Street West
Toronto, ON
M6S 1N9
416-760-7592

346 Queen Street West
Toronto, ON
M5V 2A2
416-979-8140

2619 Yonge Street
Toronto, ON
M4P 2J1
416-482-8480

120 Yorkville Ave.
Toronto, ON
M5R 1C2
416-961-3053

120 Kent
Charlottetown, PEI
C1A 8R8
902-569-5716

425 rue Principale
Hudson, QC
J0P 1H0
450-458-1717

Carrefour Laval
3035 boul. Le Carrefour
Laval, QC
H7T 1C7
450-973-9961

108 Gallery Square
Montréal, QC
H3C 3R3
514-846-1091

1500 Ave. Mc-Gill College
Montréal, QC
H3A 3J5
514-847-5307

3941 rue St-Denis
Montréal, QC
H2W 2M4
514-842-7693

118 ch. Kandahar
Mt-Tremblant, QC
J0T 1Z0
819-681-6363

1051 rue Laurier Ouest
Outremont, QC
H2V 2L2
514-273-9700

6815 Rte. Trans-Canadienne
Pte-Claire, QC
H9R 5J1
514-426-1616

Place de la Cité
2600 boul. Laurier
Ste-Foy, QC
G1V 4T3
418-651-1305

1150 rue St-Jean
Vieux-Quebec, QC
G1R 1S6
418-692-0398

1353 Ave. Greene
Westmount, QC
H3Z 2A5
514-935-4361

# Retail Outlets for April Cornell Products in the United States

Peet's Coffee & Tea
Stores Nationwide
www.peets.com
800-999-2132

Sur La Table Catalog
Stores Nationwide
www.surlatable.com
800-243-0852

Sutton Place/Hayday
Stores throughout the
Northeast

A Place Remembered
309 A De La Mare Ave.
Fairhope, AL 36532
251-928-8948

Plaza Design
808 G. Street
Arcata, CA 95521
707-822-7732

Garrett Hardware
1340 Healdsburg Avenue
Healdsburg CA 95448
707-433-5593

Hiatt & Peek
6445 E. Pacific Coast Hwy
Long Beach, CA 90803
562-594-6255

Tony Matthews
447 Main Street
Placerville, CA 95667
530-626-9161

Donna's Designs
1366 S. Main Street
Salinas, CA 93901
831-206-6096

Casa Casa
1355 Lincoln Ave.
San Jose, CA 95125
408-298-2272

Mountain Hardware
11320 Donner Pass Road
Truckee, CA 96160
530-587-4844

Posh
1220 S. Liberty Point Blvd
Pueblo West, CO 81007
719-647-2714

Portabella
1 Main Street
Essex, CT 06426
860-767-6883

White Flower Farm
Route 63
Litchfield, CT 06759
860-496-9624

White Flower Farm
30 Irene Street
Torrington, CT 06790
860-496-9624

Betsy's Sunflowers
14 Avenue D
Apalachicola, FL 32320
850-653-9144

April And Ezzie's
1415 Timberlane Road
Tallahassee, FL 32312
850-894-0448

Monet's Garden at the
Greenery
236 City Circle
Peachtree City, GA 30269
770-486-6706

Hen House
403 Grand Ave.
Spencer, IA 51301
712-262-4839

April's Drawers
821 West Idaho
Boise, ID 83702
208-343-3672

Anna Leigh's
210 Sherman Ave.
Coeur D'Alene Resort Plz
Coeur D'Alene, ID 83814
208-664-3272

Vie Paysanne
227 Lee Lane
Covington, LA 70433
985-893-1013

Epiphany
432 Main Street
Chatham, MA 02633
508-945-4931

Bean And Cod
140 Main Street
Falmouth, MA 02540
508-548-8840

Handblock
4 South Water Street
Nantucket, MA 02554
508-228-4500

Homespun Gatherings
38 Merrimac Street
Newburyport, MA 01950
978-465-1991

Longmeadow Flowers & Gifts
57 Allen Street
Springfield, MA 01108
413-739-6941

Wenham Exchange
4 Monument Street
Wenham, MA 01984
978-468-1235

Baskets Baubles And Beans
1 Lan Drive
Primrose Park
Westford, MA 01886
978-692-9899

Catch Can
10505 Metropolitan Ave.
Kensington, MD 20895
301-933-7862

Surroundings
246 Main Street
Lincolnville, ME 04849
207-236-8536

Horrocks Farm Market Inc.
235 Capital SW
Battle Creek, MI 49015
616-966-3200

Horrocks Kentwood
4455 Breton Ave. SE
Kentwood, MI 49508
616-455-7998

General Store Of Minnetonka
14401 Hwy. 7
Minnetonka, MN 55345
952-935-7131

Silver Dollar City
The Grand Village Shops
399 Indian Point Road
Branson, MO 65616
417-338-2611

Brown Derby
2023 S. Glenstone
Springfield, MO 65804
417-881-1215

Red Rooster Trading
Company
301 N. Higgins Ave.
Missoula, MT 59802
406-543-7777

Bloomfield's Dish Barn
Route 4, Box 54A
Flat Rock, NC 28731
828-693-3350

C Beston & Company
7 Lebanon Street
Hanover, NH 03755
603-653-0123

Gabrielle & Co.
Stainton Square
810 Asbury Ave
Ocean City, NJ 08226
609-399-1008

Hannah's & Sarah's
Country Crossroads
74 E. Main Street
Ramsey, NJ 07446
201-236-6444

Clay Angel
125 Lincoln Ave.
Santa Fe, NM 87501
505-988-4800

Parkleigh
215 Park Ave.
Rochester, NY 14607
585-244-4842

Nostalgia
432 Broadway
Saratoga Springs, NY 12866
518-584-4665

Summerfield Lane
386 Broadway
Saratoga Springs, NY 12866
518-584-1266

O Suzanna
108 Main Street
Westhampton Beach, NY
11978
631-288-2202

Maggie Rhodes
248 E. 5th Ave.
Eugene, OR 97401
541-686-3329

Lupine Annie's
Home & Garden Mercantile
120A Hwy. 82
Lostine, OR 97857
541-569-5197

Dieci Soli
304 Northwest 11th Ave.
Portland, OR 97209
503-222-4221

The Wild Hare
321 W. Cascade
Sisters, OR 97759
541-549-6061

In The Mood
523 Main Street
Bethlehem, PA 18018
610-694-9442

Waterloo Gardens
200 North Whitford Road
Exton, PA 19341
610-293-0800

Runcible Spoon
180 Bellevue Ave.
Newport, RI 02840
401-831-6600

Wickford Gourmet & Kitchen
21 W. Main Street
Wickford, RI 02852
401-295-9790

The Moose's Antlers
517 Elm Street
Graham, TX 76450
940-549-6315

The Happy Cook
5714 Grove Ave.
Richmond, VA 23229
804-923-0897

Moose River Lake & Lodge
Store
370 Railroad Street
St. Johnsbury, VT 05819
802-751-8518

Maggie Rhodes
16527 NE 74th Street
Redmond, WA 98052
425-885-0185

Island Child
Grand Harbor Shopping
Center
Red Bay
Grand Cayman, BWI
345-947-8517

# Retail Outlets for April Cornell Products in Canada

Chintz
1238 11th Ave. SW
Calgary, AB
T3C 0M4
403-245-3449

Chateau Country Lace
3B Parkdale Cr. NW
Calgary, AB
T2N 3E6
403-270-9666

Chintz
10502 105th Ave. SW
Edmonton, AB
T5H 0K8
780-428-8181

Holland's Home Fashions
Ltd.
1421 3rd Ave. South
Lethbridge, AB
T1J 0K7
403-327-4475

The Butchart Gardens
800 Benvenuto Ave.
Brentwood Bay, BC
V8M 1J8
250-652-4422

The Laughing Moon
4600 Lakeshore Road
Kelowna, BC
V1W 1X4
250-764-0664

Dandy Lines
1275 4th Ave.
Prince George, BC
V2L 3J9
250-563-3438

Chintz
950 Homer Street
Vancouver, BC
V6B 2W7
604-689-2022

Chintz
1720 Store Street
Victoria, BC
V8W 1V5
250-388-0996

Eloise
83 York Street
Fredericton, NB
E2L 1G2
506-453-7715

The Curiosity Shop
315 Main Street
Antigonish, NS
P2G 2C3
902-863-3559

La Cache
Sunnyside Mall
1595 Bedford Highway
Bedford, NS
B4A 3Y4
902-835-0078

Timely Accents
384 George Street North
Peterborough, ON
K9H 3R5
705-741-1530

Settlement House
183 Queen Street
Port Perry, ON
L9L 1B8
905-985-8234

La Cache
136 Front Street North
Sarnia, ON
N7T 5S3
519-383-1477

La Cache
87 Ontario Street
Stratford, ON
N5A 3H1
519-273-6617

Beach Stoneworks
2216 Queen Street East
Toronto, ON
M4E 1E9
416-698-6007

Literie Clair de Lune
1401 Boul. Talbot
Place du Royaume
Chicoutimi, QC
G7H 5N6
418-693-0820

Passerose
88 Main Street
North Hatley, QC
J0B 2C0
819-842-4722

Home Again Broadway
725 Broadway Ave.
Saskatoon, SK
S7N 1B3
306-652-7626

The Treasure Chest
4200 4th Ave.
Whitehorse, YT
Y1A 1K1
867-667-2759

# Index